Robert Dodsley

A Collection of Poems

Vol. II

Robert Dodsley

A Collection of Poems
Vol. II

ISBN/EAN: 9783744710749

Printed in Europe, USA, Canada, Australia, Japan

Cover: Foto ©Thomas Meinert / pixelio.de

More available books at **www.hansebooks.com**

A

COLLECTION of POEMS.

A NEW EDITION CORRECTED;

WITH NOTES.

VOL. II.

A COLLECTION OF POEMS

IN SIX VOLUMES.

BY

SEVERAL HANDS.

WITH NOTES.

LONDON:
Printed for J. DODSLEY, in PALL-MALL.
MDCCLXXXII.

BR
D6
1782
v.2

THE PROGRESS of LOVE.
IN FOUR ECLOGUES.
By GEORGE LORD LYTTELTON [a].

UNCERTAINTY. Eclogue I.
To Mr. POPE.

POPE, to whose reed beneath the beechen shade,
  The Nymphs of Thames a pleas'd attention paid;

[a] This noble author was born in the year 1709. He was the eldest son of Sir Thomas Lyttelton, of Hagley in Worcestershire, and received his education at Eton, where he was so much distinguished, that

While yet thy Muse, content with humbler praise,
Warbled in Windsor's grove her sylvan lays;
Though now sublimely borne on Homer's wing,
Of glorious wars, and godlike chiefs she sing:
Wilt thou with me re-visit once again
The crystal fountain, and the flow'ry plain?
Wilt thou, indulgent, hear my verse relate
The various changes of a lover's state;
And while each turn of passion I pursue,
Ask thy own heart if what I tell be true?

 To the green margin of a lonely wood,
Whose pendent shades o'erlook'd a silver flood,
Young Damon came, unknowing where he stray'd,
Full of the image of his beauteous maid:
His flock far off, unfed, untended lay,
To every savage a defenceless prey;
No sense of int'rest could their master move,
And every care seem'd trifling now but Love.

his exercises were recommended as models to his school-fellows. From Eton he went to Christ Church, Oxford, but staid there only a short time. He then travelled through France and Italy, and, soon after his return to England, in 1735, obtained a seat in Parliament, where he became a violent opposer of Sir Robert Walpole's administration. In the year 1741, he married Miss Lucy Fortescue, the lady to whom several of the following Poems are addressed; and in 1744, was made one of the Lords of the Treasury. He frequently after this period was in place, and supported the measures of the Court. In 1756, he was created a Peer; and died at Hagley, August 22, 1773, aged 64 years.

Awhile

Awhile in pensive silence he remain'd,
But though his voice was mute, his looks complain'd;
At length the thoughts within his bosom pent,
Forc'd his unwilling tongue to give them vent.

 Ye Nymphs, he cry'd, ye Dryads, who so long
Have favour'd Damon, and inspir'd his song;
For whom, retir'd, I shun the gay resorts
Of sportful cities, and of pompous courts;
In vain I bid the restless world adieu,
To seek tranquillity and peace with you.
Though wild Ambition and destructive Rage
No factions here can form, no wars can wage;
Though Envy frowns not on your humble shades,
Nor Calumny your innocence invades,
Yet cruel Love, that troubler of the breast,
Too often violates your boasted rest;
With inbred storms disturbs your calm retreat,
And taints with bitterness each rural sweet.

 Ah luckless day! when first with fond surprize
On Delia's face I fix'd my eager eyes;
Then in wild tumults all my soul was tost,
Then reason, liberty, at once were lost:
And every wish, and thought, and care was gone,
But what my heart employ'd on her alone.
Then too she smil'd: can smiles our peace destroy,
Those lovely children of Content and Joy?
How can soft pleasure and tormenting woe,
From the same spring at the same moment flow?

Unhappy

Unhappy boy, thefe vain enquiries ceafe,
Thought could not guard, nor will reftore thy peace:
Indulge the frenzy that thou muft endure,
And footh the pain thou know'ft not how to cure.
Come, flatt'ring Memory, and tell my heart
How kind fhe was, and with what pleafing art
She ftrove its fondeft wifhes to obtain,
Confirm her pow'r, and fafter bind my chain.
If on the green we danc'd, a mirthful band;
To me alone fhe gave her willing hand;
Her partial tafte, if e'er I touch'd the lyre,
Still in my fong found fomething to admire.
By none but her my crook with flow'rs was crown'd,
By none but her my brows with ivy bound:
The world that Damon was her choice believ'd,
The world, alas! like Damon was deceiv'd.
When laft I faw her, and declar'd my fire,
In words as foft as paffion could infpire,
Coldly fhe heard, and full of fcorn withdrew,
Without one pitying glance, one fweet adieu.
The frighted hind, who fees his ripen'd corn
Up from the roots by fudden tempeft torn,
Whofe faireft hopes deftroy'd and blafted lie,
Feels not fo keen a pang of grief as I.
Ah! how have I deferv'd, inhuman maid,
To have my faithful fervice thus repay'd?
Were all the marks of kindnefs I receiv'd,
But dreams of joy, that charm'd me and deceiv'd?

Or did you only nurse my growing love,
That with more pain I might your hatred prove?
Sure guilty treachery no place could find
In such a gentle, such a gen'rous mind:
A maid brought up the woods and wilds among,
Could ne'er have learnt the art of courts so young:
No; let me rather think her anger feign'd;
Still let me hope my Delia may be gain'd;
'Twas only modesty that seem'd disdain,
And her heart suffer'd when she gave me pain.

   Pleas'd with this flattering thought, the love-sick boy
Felt the faint dawnings of a doubtful joy;
Back to his flock more chearful he return'd,
When now the setting sun less fiercely burn'd;
Blue vapours rose along the mazy rills,
And light's last blushes ting'd the distant hills.

HOPE. Eclogue II.

To Mr. DODDINGTON,

Afterwards Lord MELCOMBE.

HEAR, DODDINGTON, the notes that shepherds sing,
Notes soft as those of nightingales in spring;
Nor Pan, nor Phœbus tune the shepherd's reed;
From Love alone our tender lays proceed:
Love warms our fancy with enliv'ning fires,
Refines our genius, and our verse inspires:
From him Theocritus, on Enna's plains,
Learnt the wild sweetness of his Doric strains;
Virgil by him was taught the moving art,
That charm'd each ear, and soften'd every heart:
O would'st thou quit the pride of courts, and deign
To dwell with us upon the vocal plain,
Thee too his pow'r should reach, and every shade
Resound the praises of thy fav'rite maid;
Thy pipe our rural concert would improve,
And we should learn of thee to please and love.

Damon no longer sought the silent shade,
No more in unfrequented paths he stray'd,

But call'd the nymphs to hear his jocund song,
And told his joy to all the ruſtic throng.

  Bleſt be the hour, he ſaid, that happy hour,
When firſt I own'd my Delia's gentle pow'r;
Then gloomy diſcontent and pining care
Forſook my breaſt, and left ſoft wiſhes there:
Soft wiſhes there they left, and gay deſires,
Delightful languors, and tranſporting fires.
Where yonder limes combine to form a ſhade,
Theſe eyes firſt gaz'd upon the charming maid;
There ſhe appear'd, on that auſpicious day,
When ſwains their ſportive rites to Bacchus pay:
She led the dance—heavens! with what grace ſhe mov'd!
Who could have ſeen her then, and not have lov'd?
I ſtrove not to reſiſt ſo ſweet a flame,
But glory'd in a happy captive's name;
Nor would I now, could Love permit, be free,
But leave to brutes their ſavage liberty.

  And art thou then, fond ſwain, ſecure of joy?
Can no reverſe thy flatt'ring bliſs deſtroy?
Has treach'rous Love no torment yet in ſtore?
Or haſt thou never prov'd his fatal pow'r?
Whence flow'd thoſe tears that late bedew'd thy cheek?
Why ſigh'd thy heart as if it ſtrove to break?
Why were the deſart rocks invok'd to hear
The plaintive accents of thy ſad deſpair?
From Delia's rigour all thoſe pains aroſe,
Delia, who now compaſſionates my woes,

Who bids me hope; and in that charming word
Has peace and transport to my soul restor'd.

Begin, my pipe, begin the gladsome lay;
A kiss from Delia shall thy music pay;
A kiss obtain'd 'twixt struggling and consent,
Giv'n with forc'd anger, and disguis'd content:
No laureat wreaths I ask to bind my brows,
Such as the Muse on lofty bards bestows;
Let other swains to praise or fame aspire:
I from her lips my recompence require.

Hark how the bees with murmurs fill the plain,
While every flow'r of every sweet they drain;
See, how beneath yon hillock's shady steep,
The shelter'd herds on flow'ry couches sleep;
Nor bees, nor herds, are half so blest as I,
If with my fond desires my Love comply:
From Delia's lips a sweeter honey flows,
And on her bosom dwells more soft repose.

Ah how, my dear, shall I deserve thy charms?
What gift can bribe thee to my longing arms?
A bird for thee in silken bands I hold,
Whose yellow plumage shines like polish'd gold;
From distant isles the lovely stranger came,
And bears the Fortunate Canaries name;
In all our woods none boasts so sweet a note,
Not ev'n the nightingale's melodious throat.
Accept of this; and could I add beside
What wealth the rich Peruvian mountains hide;

If

If all the gems in Eastern rocks were mine,
On thee alone their glitt'ring pride should shine.
But if thy mind no gifts have pow'r to move,
Phœbus himself shall leave th' Aonian grove;
The tuneful Nine, who never sue in vain,
Shall come sweet suppliants for their fav'rite swain.
For him each blue-ey'd Naiad of the flood,
For him each green-hair'd sister of the wood,
Whom oft beneath fair Cynthia's gentle ray
His music calls to dance the night away.
And you, fair nymphs, companions of my Love,
With whom she joys the cowslip meads to rove,
I beg you recommend my faithful flame,
And let her often hear her shepherd's name;
Shade all my faults from her enquiring sight,
And shew my merits in the fairest light;
My pipe your kind assistance shall repay,
And ev'ry friend shall claim a diff'rent lay.

 But see! in yonder glade the heav'nly fair
Enjoys the fragrance of the breezy air—
Ah, thither let me fly with eager feet;
Adieu, my pipe, I go my Love to meet—
O may I find her as we parted last,
And may each future hour be like the past!
So shall the whitest lamb these pastures feed,
Propitious Venus, on thy altars bleed.

          J E A-

JEALOUSY. Eclogue III.

To Mr. EDWARD WALPOLE,

Now Sir EDWARD WALPOLE, second Son to Sir ROBERT WALPOLE, Earl of Orford.

THE gods, O WALPOLE, give no bliss sincere:
Wealth is disturb'd by care, and pow'r by fear.
Of all the passions that employ the mind,
In gentle love the sweetest joys we find;
Yet ev'n those joys dire Jealousy molests,
And blackens each fair image in our breasts.
O may the warmth of thy too tender heart
Ne'er feel the sharpness of his venom'd dart;
For thy own quiet think thy mistress just,
And wisely take thy happiness on trust.

Begin, my Muse, and Damon's woes rehearse,
In wildest numbers and disorder'd verse.

On a romantic mountain's airy head
(While browzing goats at ease around him fed)
Anxious he lay, with jealous cares oppress'd;
Distrust and anger lab'ring in his breast—
The vale beneath a pleasing prospect yields,
Of verdant meads and cultivated fields;

Through

Through thefe a river rolls its winding flood,
Adorn'd with various tufts of rifing wood ;
Here half conceal'd in trees a cottage ftands,
A caftle there the op'ning plain commands,
Beyond, a town with glitt'ring fpires is crown'd,
And diftant hills the wide horizon bound ;
So charming was the fcene, awhile the fwain
Beheld delighted, and forgot his pain ;
But foon the ftings infix'd within his heart,
With cruel force renew'd their raging fmart :
His flow'ry wreath, which long with pride he wore,
The gift of Delia, from his brows he tore :
Then cry'd ; May all thy charms, ungrateful maid,
Like thefe neglected rofes droop and fade ;
May angry Heav'n deform each guilty grace,
That triumphs now in that deluding face ;
Thofe alter'd looks may every fhepherd fly,
And ev'n thy Daphnis hate thee worfe than I !

 Say, thou inconftant, what has Damon done,
To lofe the heart his tedious pains had won ?
Tell me what charms you in my rival find,
Againft whofe power no ties have ftrength to bind :
Has he, like me, with long obedience ftrove,
To conquer your difdain, and merit love ?
Has he with tranfport every fmile ador'd,
And dy'd with grief at each ungentle word ?
Ah, no ! the conqueft was obtain'd with eafe :
He pleas'd you, by not ftudying to pleafe :

His carelefs indolence your pride alarm'd;
And had he lov'd you more, he lefs had charm'd.
  O pain to think, another fhall poffefs
Thofe balmy lips which I was wont to prefs:
Another on her panting breaft fhall lie,
And catch fweet madnefs from her fwimming eye!
I faw their friendly flocks together feed,
I faw them hand in hand walk o'er the mead:
Would my clos'd eyes had funk in endlefs night,
Ere I was doom'd to bear that hateful fight!
Where'er they pafs'd be blafted every flow'r,
And hungry wolves their helplefs flocks devour!—
Ah wretched fwain! could no examples move
Thy heedlefs heart to fhun the rage of Love?
Haft thou not heard how poor ^b Menalcas dy'd
A victim to Parthenia's fatal pride?
Dear was the youth to all the tuneful plain,
Lov'd by the nymphs, by Phœbus lov'd in vain:
Around his tomb their tears the Mufes paid,
And all things mourn'd but the relentlefs maid.
Would I could die like him, and be at peace!
Thefe torments in the quiet grave would ceafe;
There my vex'd thoughts a calm repofe would find,
And reft as if my Delia ftill were kind.
No, let me live her falfhood to upbraid;
Some god perhaps my juft revenge will aid.—

b See Mr. Gay's Dione.

Alas!

Alas! what aid, fond swain, wouldst thou receive?
Could thy heart bear to see its Delia grieve?
Protect her, Heav'n, and let her never know
The slightest part of hapless Damon's woe:
I ask no vengeance from the pow'rs above;
All I implore is never more to love—
Let me this fondness from my bosom tear,
Let me forget that e'er I thought her fair.
Come, cool Indifference, and heal my breast;
Wearied, at length I seek thy downy rest:
No turbulence of passion shall destroy
My future ease with flatt'ring hopes of joy.
Hear, mighty Pan, and all ye Sylvans hear;
What by your guardian deities I swear;
No more my eyes shall view her fatal charms,
No more I'll court the trait'ress to my arms;
Not all her arts my steady soul shall move,
And she shall find that Reason conquers Love.—

 Scarce had he spoke, when through the lawn below
Alone he saw the beauteous Delia go;
At once transported he forgot his vow,
(Such perjuries the laughing gods allow)
Down the steep hills with ardent haste he flew;
He found her kind, and soon believ'd her true.

POSSESSION. Eclogue IV.

To Lord COBHAM [a].

COBHAM, to thee this rural lay I bring,
Whose guiding judgment gives me skill to sing;
Though far unequal to those polish'd strains,
With which thy Congreve charm'd the list'ning plains,
Yet shall its music please thy partial ear,
And sooth thy breast with thoughts that once were dear;
Recall those years which time has thrown behind,
When smiling Love with Honour shar'd thy mind:
The sweet remembrance shall thy youth restore,
Fancy again shall run past pleasures o'er,
And while in Stow's enchanting walks you stray,
This theme may help to cheat the summer's day.
   Beneath the covert of a myrtle wood,
To Venus rais'd, a rustic altar stood,
To Venus and to Hymen, there combin'd,
In friendly league to favour human kind.
With wanton Cupids in that happy shade,
The gentle Virtues, and mild Wisdom play'd.

[a] The Author's Uncle. He died at Stow, September 13, 1749.

Nor there in sprightly Pleasure's genial train,
Lurk'd sick Disgust, or late-repenting Pain,
Nor Force, nor Int'rest, join'd unwilling hands,
But Love consenting ty'd the blissful bands.
Thither with glad devotion Damon came,
To thank the pow'rs who bless'd his faithful flame;
Two milk-white doves he on their altar laid,
And thus to both his grateful homage paid:
Hail, bounteous god, before whose hallow'd shrine
My Delia vow'd to be for ever mine,
While glowing in her cheeks, with tender love,
Sweet virgin modesty reluctant strove:
And hail to thee, fair queen of young desires,
Long shall my heart preserve thy pleasing fires,
Since Delia now can all its warmth return,
As fondly languish, and as fiercely burn.

O the dear gloom of last propitious night!
O shade more charming than the fairest light!
Then in my arms I clasp'd the melting maid,
Then all my pains one moment overpaid;
Then first the sweet excess of bliss I prov'd,
Which none can taste but who like me have lov'd.
Thou too, bright goddess, once in Ida's grove,
Didst not disdain to meet a shepherd's love,
With him while frisking lambs around you play'd,
Conceal'd you sported in the secret shade;
Scarce could Anchises' raptures equal mine,
And Delia's beauties only yield to thine.

What are you now, my once most-valu'd joys?
Insipid trifles all, and childish toys ——
Friendship itself ne'er knew a charm like this,
Nor Colin's talk could please like Delia's kiss.

   Ye Muses, skill'd in every winning art,
Teach me more deeply to engage her heart;
Ye Nymphs, to her your freshest roses bring,
And crown her with the pride of all the spring;
On all her days let health and peace attend;
May she ne'er want, nor ever lose a friend;
May some new pleasure every hour employ;
But let her Damon be her highest joy!

   With thee, my Love, for ever will I stay,
All night caress thee, and admire all day;
In the same field our mingled flocks we'll feed,
To the same spring our thirsty heifers lead,
Together will we share the harvest toils,
Together press the vine's autumnal spoils;
Delightful state, where peace and love combine,
To bid our tranquil days unclouded shine!
Here limpid fountains roll through flow'ry meads,
Here rising forests lift their verdant heads;
Here let me wear my careless life away,
And in thy arms insensibly decay.

   When late old age our heads shall silver o'er,
And our slow pulses dance with joy no more;
When time no longer will thy beauties spare,
And only Damon's eye shall think thee fair;

                                   Then

Then may the gentle hand of welcome death,
At one soft stroke deprive us both of breath;
May we beneath one common stone be laid,
And the same cypress both our ashes shade.
Perhaps some friendly Muse, in tender verse,
Shall deign our faithful passion to rehearse,
And future ages with just envy mov'd,
Be told how Damon and his Delia lov'd.

SOLILOQUY

Of a BEAUTY in the COUNTRY.

Written at Eton School. By the Same.

'TWAS night; and FLAVIA to her room retir'd,
    With ev'ning chat and sober reading tir'd;
There melancholy, pensive, and alone,
She meditates on the forsaken town:
On her rais'd arm reclin'd her drooping head,
She sigh'd, and thus in plaintive accents said:
    " Ah, what avails it to be young and fair,
    " To move with negligence, to dress with care?
    " What worth have all the charms our pride can boast,
    " If all in envious solitude are lost?
                                               " Where

" Where none admire, 'tis useless to excel;
" Where none are Beaus, 'tis vain to be a Belle:
" Beauty, like wit, to judges should be shewn;
" Both most are valu'd where they best are known.
" With every grace of nature, or of art,
" We cannot break one stubborn country heart:
" The brutes, insensible, our pow'r defy:
" To love exceeds a 'Squire's capacity.
" The town, the court, is Beauty's proper sphere;
" That is our heav'n, and we are angels There:
" In that gay circle thousand Cupids rove,
" The court of Britain is the court of Love.
" How has my conscious heart with triumph glow'd,
" How have my sparkling eyes their transport shew'd,
" At each distinguish'd birth-night ball, to see
" The homage due to empire, paid to me!
" When every eye was fix'd on me alone,
" And dreaded mine more than the monarch's frown:
" When rival statesmen for my favour strove,
" Less jealous in their pow'r, than in their love.
" Chang'd is the scene; and all my glories die,
" Like flow'rs transplanted to a colder sky;
" Lost is the dear delight of giving pain,
" The tyrant joy of hearing slaves complain.
" In stupid indolence my life is spent,
" Supinely calm, and dully innocent:
" Unblest I wear my useless time away;
" Sleep (wretched maid!) all night, and dream all day;

" Go

" Go at set hours to dinner and to prayer;
" For dulness ever must be regular.
" Now with mamma at tedious whist I play;
" Now without scandal drink insipid tea;
" Or in the garden breathe the country air;
" Secure from meeting any Tempter there:
" From books to work, from work to books I rove,
" And am (alas!) at leisure to improve!
" Is this the life a Beauty ought to lead?
" Were eyes so radiant only made to read?
" These fingers, at whose touch ev'n age would glow,
" Are these of use for nothing but to sew?
" Sure erring Nature never could design
" To form a housewife in a mould like mine!
" O Venus, queen and guardian of the fair,
" Attend propitious to thy vot'ry's pray'r:
" Let me revisit the dear town again:
" Let me be seen!—could I that wish obtain,
" All other wishes my own pow'r would gain."

BLENHEIM,

Written at the University of OXFORD in the Year 1727.

By the Same.

PARENT of arts, whose skilful hand first taught
The tow'ring pile to rise, and form'd the plan
With fair proportion; architect divine,
Minerva, thee to my advent'rous lyre
Assistant I invoke, that means to sing
BLENHEIM, thou monument of British fame,
Thy glorious work! for thou the lofty tow'rs
Didst to his virtue raise, whom oft thy shield
In peril guarded, and thy wisdom steer'd
Through all the storms of war.—Thee too I call,
Thalia, sylvan Muse, who lov'st to rove
Along the shady paths and verdant bow'rs
Of Woodstock's happy grove: there tuning sweet
Thy rural pipe, while all the Dryad train
Attentive listen; let thy warbling song
Paint with melodious praise the pleasing scene,
And equal these to Pindus' honour'd shades.

When Europe freed, confess'd the saving pow'r
Of MARLB'ROUGH's hand; Britain, who sent him forth

Chief of confed'rate hosts, to fight the cause
Of Liberty and Justice, grateful rais'd
This palace, sacred to her Leader's fame;
A trophy of success; with spoils adorn'd
Of conquer'd towns, and glorying in the name
Of that auspicious field, where CHURCHILL's sword
Vanquish'd the might of Gallia, and chastis'd
Rebel Bavar.—Majestic in its strength
Stands the proud dome, and speaks its great design.

    Hail happy Chief, whose valour could deserve
Reward so glorious! grateful nation hail,
Who paid'st his service with so rich a meed!
Which most shall I admire, which worthiest praise,
The Hero or the People? Honour doubts,
And weighs their virtues in an equal scale.
[a] Not thus Germania pays th' uncancell'd debt
Of gratitude to us.——Blush, Cæsar, blush,

---

[a] About the time this poem was written, the friendship between England and the Empire had much abated. In the year 1724, a congress had been held at Cambray, where, while France and the maritime powers were taking all imaginable pains to fix the general tranquillity of Europe upon a solid basis, the courts of Vienna and Madrid entered into a private negotiation, which terminated soon after in two several treaties of alliance and commerce between the two courts, so much to the advantage of the emperor, and so utterly inconsistent with the interest of France, and the maritime powers, that they found themselves under an absolute necessity of entering into a treaty for their own security, which was accordingly signed and concluded in 1725 at Hanover.

When thou behold'st thefe tow'rs, ingrate, to thee
A monument of fhame.   Canft thou forget
Whence they are nam'd, and what an Englifh arm
Did for thy throne that day ? But we difdain
Or to upbraid, or imitate thy guilt.
Steel thy obdurate heart againft the fenfe
Of obligation infinite, and know,
Britain, like Heav'n, protects a thanklefs world
For her own glory, nor expects reward.

 Pleas'd with the noble theme, her tafk the Mufe
Purfues untir'd, and through the palace roves
With ever-new delight.   The tap'ftry rich
With gold, and gay with all the beauteous paint
Of various-colour'd filks, difpos'd with fkill,
Attracts her curious eye.   Here Ifter rolls
His purple wave ; and there the Granic flood
With paffing fquadrons foams: here hardy Gaul
Flies from the fword of Britain ; there to Greece
Effeminate Perfia yields —In arms oppos'd
MARLB'ROUGH and ALEXANDER vie for fame
With glorious competition ; equal both
In valour and in fortune, but their praife
Be diff'rent, for with diff'rent views they fought ;
This to *fubdue*, and that to *free* mankind.

 Now through the ftately portals iffuing forth,
The Mufe to fof er glories turns, and feeks
The woodland fhade, delighted.   Not the vale
Of Tempé, fam'd in fong, or Ida's grove

Such

Such beauty boasts. Amid the mazy gloom
Of this romantic wilderness once stood
The bow'r of Rosamonda, hapless fair,
Sacred to grief and love: the crystal fount
In which she us'd to bathe her beauteous limbs
Still warbling flows, pleas'd to reflect the face
Of SPENCER[b], lovely maid, when tir'd she sits
Beside its flow'ry brink, and views those charms,
Which only Rosamond could once excel.
But see where flowing with a nobler stream,
A limpid lake of purest waters rolls
Beneath the wide-stretch'd arch, stupendous work,
Through which the Danube might collected pour
His spacious urn! Silent awhile and smooth
The current glides, 'till with an headlong force
Broke and disorder'd, down the steep it falls
In loud cascades; the silver-sparkling foam
Glitters relucent in the dancing ray.

In these retreats repos'd the mighty soul
Of CHURCHILL, from the toils of war and state,
Splendidly private, and the tranquil joy
Of contemplation felt, while BLENHEIM's dome
Triumphal, ever in his mind renew'd
The mem'ry of his fame, and sooth'd his thoughts

---

[b] Lady Diana Spencer, youngest daughter of the earl of Sunderland, afterwards married to John, fourth duke of Bedford. She died September 27, 1735.

With pleasing record of his glorious deeds.
So by the rage of faction, home recall'd,
Lucullus, while he wag'd successful war
Against the pride of Asia, and the pow'r
Of Mithridates, whose aspiring mind
No losses could subdue, enrich'd with spoils
Of conquer'd nations, back return'd to Rome,
And in magnificent retirement past
The evening of his life.—But not alone,
In the calm shades of honourable ease,
Great MARLB'ROUGH peaceful dwelt: Indulgent Heav'n
Gave a companion to his softer hours,
With whom conversing, he forgot all change
Of fortune, or of taste, and in her mind
Found greatness equal to his own, and lov'd
Himself in her.—Thus each by each admir'd,
In mutual honour, mutual fondness join'd:
Like two fair stars with intermingled light,
In friendly union they together shone,
Aiding each other's brightness, 'till the cloud
Of night eternal quench'd the beams of one.
Thee, CHURCHILL, first the ruthless hand of death [c]
Tore from thy consort's side, and call'd thee hence
To the sublimer seats of joy and love;

[c] The duke of Marlborough died at Windsor, June 16, 1722, having some years survived his mental faculties.

Where fate again shall join her soul to thine,
Who now, regardful of thy fame, erects
The column to thy praise, and sooths her woe
With pious honours to thy sacred name
Immortal. Lo! where tow'ring on the height
Of yon aërial pillar proudly stands
Thy image, like a guardian god, sublime,
And awes the subject plain: beneath his feet,
The German eagles spread their wings, his hand
Grasps Victory, its slave. Such was thy brow
Majestic, such thy martial port, when Gaul
Fled from thy frown, and in the Danube sought
A refuge from thy sword.—There, where the field
Was deepest stain'd with gore, on Hochstet's plain,
The theatre of thy glory, once was rais'd [d]
A meaner trophy, by th' Imperial hand;
Extorted gratitude; which now the rage
Of Malice impotent, beseeming ill
A regal breast, has levell'd to the ground:
Mean insult! this with better auspices
Shall stand on British earth, to tell the world

---

[d] Voltaire observes, " It has been said and affirmed in most histories,
" that the emperor caused a monument of this defeat to be raised in the
" plains of Blenheim, with an inscription extremely satirical upon
" Lewis. But such a monument never existed: nor was there one any
" where but in England, which was erected in honour of the duke of
" Marlborough. Age of Lewis the XIVth, c. 18.

How

How MARLB'ROUGH fought, for whom, and how repay'd
His services.   Nor shall the constant love
[e] Of her who rais'd this monument be lost
In dark oblivion : that shall be the theme
Of future bards in ages yet unborn,
Inspir'd with Chaucer's fire, who in these groves
First tun'd the British harp, and little deem'd
His humble dwelling should the neighbour be
Of BLENHEIM, house superb ; to which the throng
Of travellers approaching, shall not pass
His roof unnoted, but respectful hail
With rev'rence due.   Such honour does the Muse
Obtain her fav'rites——But the noble pile
(My theme) demands my voice——O shade ador'd,
MARLB'ROUGH ! who now above the starry sphere
Dwell'st in the palaces of heav'n, enthron'd
Amongst the demi-gods, deign to defend
This thy abode, while present here below,
And sacred still to thy immortal fame,
With tutelary care.   Preserve it safe
From Time's destroying hand, and cruel stroke
Of factious Envy's more relentless rage.
Here may, long ages hence, the British youth,

---

[e] The obelisk erected at Blenheim, by the dutchess Dowager of Marlborough, has inscribed on it an account of the duke's actions and character, written by Dr. Hare, bishop of Chichester.

When

When honour calls them to the field of war,
Behold the trophies which thy valour rais'd;
The proud rewa d of thy succefsful toils
For Europe's freedom, and Britannia's fame:
That fir'd with gen'rous envy, they may dare
To emulate thy deeds.——So fhall thy name,
Dear to thy country, ftill infpire her fons
With martial virtue; and to high attempts
Excite their arms, 'till other battles won,
And nations fav'd, new monuments require,
And other BLENHEIMS fhall adorn the land.

TO THE
Reverend Dr. AYSCOUGH[a]
at OXFORD.

Written from PARIS in the Year 1728.

By the Same.

SAY, dearest friend, how roll thy hours away?
What pleasing study cheats the tedious day?
Dost thou the sacred volumes oft explore
Of wise Antiquity's immortal lore,
Where virtue by the charms of wit refin'd,
At once exalts and polishes the mind?
How diff'rent from our modern guilty art,
Which pleases only to corrupt the heart;

---

[a] Preceptor to his Majesty George the third. He was tutor to Lord Lyttelton, at Oxford, and afterwards, by marrying a sister of his pupil's, became brother-in-law to him. At the time of his death, which happened 15th August 1763, he was Dean of Bristol.

Whose curs'd refinements odious Vice adorn,
And teach to honour what we ought to scorn!
Dost thou in sage Historians joy to see
How Roman Greatness rose with Liberty;
How the same hands that tyrants durst controul,
Their empire stretch'd from Atlas to the Pole;
'Till wealth and conquest into slaves refin'd
The proud luxurious masters of mankind?
Dost thou in letter'd Greece each charm admire,
Each grace, each virtue Freedom could inspire;
Yet in her troubled states see all the woes,
And all the crimes that giddy Faction knows;
'Till rent by parties, by corruption sold,
Or weakly careless, or too rashly bold,
She sunk beneath a mitigated doom,
The slave and tut'ress of protecting Rome?

 Does calm philosophy her aid impart,
To guide the passions, and to mend the heart?
Taught by her precepts, hast thou learnt the end
To which alone the wise their studies bend;
For which alone by nature were design'd
The pow'rs of thought—to benefit mankind!
Not like a cloyster'd drone, to read and doze,
In undeserving, undeserv'd repose;
But reason's influence to diffuse; to clear
Th' enlighten'd world of every gloomy fear;
Dispel the mists of error, and unbind
Those pedant chains that clog the freeborn mind.

Happy

Happy who thus his leisure can employ!
He knows the purest hours of tranquil joy;
Nor vex'd with pangs that busier bosoms tear,
Nor lost to social Virtue's pleasing care;
Safe in the port, yet lab'ring to sustain
Those who still float on the tempestuous main.

   So Locke the days of studious quiet spent;
So Boyle in wisdom found divine content;
So Cambray, worthy of a happier doom,
The virtuous slave of Louis and of Rome.

   Good [b] Wor'ster thus supports his drooping age,
Far from court flatt'ry, far from party rage;

He,

---

[b] Dr. Hough, Bishop of Worcester. This venerable prelate was highly esteemed by Lord Lyttelton. In the Persian Letters, letter 56, he thus speaks of him:—"His character is so extraordinary, that not "to give it to thee, would be departing from the rule I have laid down, "to let nothing that is singular escape my notice. In the first place, "he resides constantly on his diocese, and has done so for many years: "he asks nothing of the Court for himself or family: he hoards up "no wealth for his relations; but lays out the revenues of his see in "a decent hospitality, and a charity void of ostentation. At his first "entrance into the world, he distinguished himself by a zeal for the "liberty of his country, and had a considerable share in bringing on the "Revolution that preserved it. His principles never altered by his "preferment: he never prostituted his pen, nor debased his character, "by party-disputes or blind compliance. Though he is warmly serious "in the belief of his religion, he is moderate to all who differ from "him: he knows no distinction of party, but extends his good offices

"alike

He, who in youth a tyrant's frown defy'd,
Firm and intrepid on his country's side,
Her boldest champion then, and now her mildest guide.
O gen'rous warmth! O sanctity divine!
To emulate his worth, my friend, be thine:
Learn from his life the duties of the gown;
Learn not to flatter, nor insult the crown;
Nor basely servile court the guilty great,
Nor raise the Church a rival to the State:
To Error mild, to Vice alone severe,
Seek not to spread the law of Love by Fear.
The priest, who plagues the world, can never mend:
No foe to man was e'er to God a friend:
Let reason and let virtue faith maintain,
All force but theirs is impious, weak, and vain.

   Me other cares in other climes engage,
Cares that become my birth, and suit my age;
In various knowledge to improve my youth,
And conquer Prejudice, worst foe to Truth:

" alike to Whig and Tory; a friend to virtue under any denomination;
" an enemy to vice under any colours. His health and old-age are the
" effects of a temperate life and a quiet conscience: though he is now
" some years above fourscore, nobody ever thought he lived too long,
" unless it was out of an impatience to succeed him." Dr. Hough
died March 8, 1743, aged ninety-three; having been a Bishop almost
fifty-three years.

By foreign arts domestic faults to mend,
Enlarge my notions, and my views extend;
The useful science of the world to know,
Which books can never teach, or pedants shew.
   A nation here I pity, and admire,
Whom noblest sentiments of glory fire,
Yet taught by custom's force, and bigot fear,
To serve with pride, and boast the yoke they bear:
Whose Nobles born to cringe, and to command,
In courts a mean, in camps a gen'rous band;
From each low tool of pow'r content receive
Those laws, their dreaded arms to Europe give.
Whose people vain in want, in bondage blest,
Though plunder'd, gay; industrious, though oppress'd:
With happy follies rise above their fate,
The jest and envy of each wiser state.
   Yet here the Muses deign'd awhile to sport
In the short sunshine of a fav'ring court:
Here Boileau, strong in sense, and sharp in wit,
Who from the ancients, like the ancients writ;
Permission gain'd inferior vice to blame,
By flatt'ring incense to his Master's fame.
Here Moliere, first of comic wits, excell'd
Whate'er Athenian theatres beheld;
By keen, yet decent satire skill'd to please,
With morals mirth uniting, strength with ease.
Now charm'd, I hear the bold Corneille inspire
Heroic thought with Shakspeare's force and fire;

Now

Now sweet Racine with milder influence move
The soften'd heart to Pity and to Love.
    With mingled pain and pleasure I survey
The pompous works of arbitrary sway;
Proud palaces, that drain'd the subjects' store,
Rais'd on the ruins of th' oppress'd and poor;
Where ev'n mute walls are taught to flatter state,
And painted triumphs stile Ambition GREAT [c].
With more delight those pleasing shades I view,
Where Condé from an envious court withdrew [d];
Where, sick of glory, faction, pow'r, and pride,
(Sure judge how empty all, who all had try'd)
Beneath his palms the weary Chief repos'd,
And life's great scene in quiet Virtue clos'd.
    With shame that other fam'd retreat I see
Adorn'd by Art, disgrac'd by Luxury [e];
Where Orleans [f] wasted every vacant hour
In the wild riot of unbounded pow'r.

---

[c] The victories of Louis XIV. painted in the galleries of Versailles.
[d] Chantilly.   [e] St. Cloud.
[f] The Duke of Orleans, regent of France, who died in the year 1723. The author of *The Private Life of Lewis XV.* vol. i. p. 131, says, " —that incest was a mere sport to him. In fact, if his love for the " Abbess de Chelles, his daughter, is not thoroughly confirmed, it is " difficult to deny his having been smitten with the charms of the " Dutchess of Berri, whose hands, which were the most beautiful that a " woman can possibly have had, particularly enchanted him. He " deplored her death rather as a lover in despair, than as an af-" flicted father."

Where feverish Debauch and impious Love
Stain'd the mad table and the guilty grove.
 With these amusements is thy friend detain'd,
Pleas'd and instructed in a foreign land;
Yet oft a tender wish recalls my mind
From present joys to dearer left behind:
 O native isle! fair Freedom's happiest seat!
At thought of thee my bounding pulses beat;
At thought of thee my heart impatient burns,
And all my country on my soul returns.
When shall I see thy fields, whose plenteous grain
No pow'r can ravish from th' industrious swain?
When kiss with pious love the sacred earth,
That gave a BURLEIGH, or a RUSSEL birth?
When, in the shade of laws, that long have stood,
Prop'd by their care, or strengthen'd by their blood,
Of fearless independence wisely vain,
The proudest slave of Bourbon's race disdain?
 Yet oh! what doubt, what sad presaging voice
Whispers within, and bids me not rejoice;
Bids me contemplate every state around,
From sultry Spain to Norway's icy bound;
Bids their lost rights, their ruin'd glories see;
And tells me, These, like England, once were Free.

To

To Mr. POYNTZ[a],

AMBASSADOR at the Congress of SOISSONS, in the Year 1728.

Written at PARIS. By the Same.

O Thou, whose friendship is my joy and pride,
  Whose virtues warm me, and whose precepts guide;
Thou, to whom greatness, rightly understood,
Is but a larger power of being good;
Say, Poyntz, amidst the toils of anxious state,
Does not thy secret soul desire retreat?
Dost thou not wish (the task of glory done)
Thy busy life at length might be thy own;
That to thy lov'd Philosophy resign'd,
No care might ruffle thy unbended mind?
Just is the wish. For sure the happiest meed,
To favour'd man by smiling Heav'n decreed,

---

[a] Stephen Poyntz, of Medgeham, in the county of Berks, Esq. He was afterwards preceptor to his Royal Highness the Duke of Cumberland, and at the time of his death, 17 December 1750, steward of that prince's household.

Is to reflect at ease on glorious pains,
And calmly to enjoy what Virtue gains.
 Not him I praise, who from the world retir'd,
By no enliv'ning gen'rous passion fir'd,
On flow'ry couches slumbers life away,
And gently bids his active pow'rs decay;
Who fears bright Glory's awful face to see,
And shuns Renown as much as Infamy.
But blest is he, who exercis'd in cares,
To private Leisure public Virtue bears:
Who tranquil ends the race he nobly run,
And decks Repose with trophies Labour won.
Him Honour follows to the secret shade,
And crowns propitious his declining head;
In his retreats their harps the Muses string,
For him in lays unbought spontaneous sing;
Friendship and Truth on all his moments wait,
Pleas'd with Retirement better than with State;
And round the bow'r where humbly great he lies,
Fair olives bloom, or verdant laurels rise.
 So when thy Country shall no more demand
The needful aid of thy sustaining hand;
When Peace restor'd shall on her downy wing
Secure Repose and careless Leisure bring:
Then to the shades of learned Ease retir'd,
The world forgetting, by the world admir'd,
Among thy books and friends, thou shalt possess
Contemplative and quiet happiness;

Pleas'd

Pleas'd to review a life in honour spent,
And painful merit paid with sweet content.
Yet though thy hours unclogg'd with sorrow roll,
Though wisdom calm, and science feed thy soul;
One dearer bliss remains to be possest,
That only can improve and crown the rest—

   Permit thy friend this secret to reveal,
Which thy own heart perhaps would better tell;
The point to which our sweetest passions move,
Is to be truly lov'd, and fondly love.
This is the charm that sooths the troubled breast,
Friend to our health, and author of our rest,
Bids every gloomy vexing passion fly,
And tunes each jarring string to harmony.
Ev'n while I write, the name of Love inspires
More pleasing thoughts and more enliv'ning fires;
Beneath his pow'r my raptur'd fancy glows,
And every tender verse more sweetly flows.
Dull is the privilege of living free;
Our hearts were never form'd for Liberty:
Some beauteous image well imprinted there,
Can best defend them from consuming care.
In vain to groves and gardens we retire,
And nature in her rural works admire;
Though grateful these, yet these but faintly charm,
They may delight us, but can never warm.
May some fair eyes, my friend, thy bosom fire
With pleasing pangs of ever gay desire;

And teach thee that soft science, which alone
Still to thy searching mind rests slightly known.
Thy soul, tho' great, is tender and refin'd;
To friendship sensible, to love inclin'd;
And therefore long thou canst not arm thy breast
Against the entrance of so sweet a guest.
Hear what th' inspiring Muses bid me tell;
For Heav'n shall ratify what they reveal:

 A chosen bride shall in thy arms be plac'd,
With all th' attractive charms of beauty grac'd;
Whose wit and virtue shall thy own express,
Distinguish'd only by their softer dress;
Thy greatness she, or thy retreat shall share,
Sweeten tranquillity, or soften care:
Her smiles the taste of every joy shall raise,
And add new pleasure to renown and praise;
'Till charm'd you own the truth my verse would prove,
That Happiness is near ally'd to Love.

VERSES

VERSES to be written under a Picture of Mr. POYNTZ.

By the Same.

SUCH is thy form, O Poyntz! but who shall find
A hand, or colours, to express thy mind?
A mind unmov'd by every vulgar fear,
In a false world that dares to be sincere;
Wise without art; without ambition great;
Though firm, yet pliant; active, though sedate;
With all the richest stores of Learning fraught,
Yet better still by native Prudence taught;
That, fond the griefs of the distress'd to heal,
Can pity frailties it could never feel;
That, when Misfortune fu'd, ne'er fought to know
What sect, what party, whether friend or foe;
That, fix'd on equal Virtue's temp'rate laws,
Despises calumny, and shuns applause;
That, to its own perfections singly blind,
Would for another think this praise design'd.

An Epistle to Mr. POPE.

From Rome, 1730. By the Same.

Immortal bard! for whom each Muse has wove
   The fairest garlands of th' Aonian grove;
Preserv'd, our drooping genius to restore,
When Addison and Congreve are no more.
After so many stars extinct in night,
The darken'd age's last remaining light!
To thee from Latian realms this verse is writ,
Inspir'd by memory of ancient wit;
For now no more these climes their influence boast,
Fall'n is their glory, and their virtue lost;
From Tyrants and from Priests the Muses fly,
Daughters of Reason and of Liberty:
Nor Baiæ now, nor Umbria's plain they love,
Nor on the banks of Nar, or Mincius rove;
To Thames's flow'ry borders they retire,
And kindle in thy breast the Roman fire.
So in the shades, where cheer'd with summer rays
Melodious linnets warbled sprightly lays,
Soon as the faded, falling leaves complain
Of gloomy Winter's unauspicious reign,
No tuneful voice is heard of joy or love,
But mournful silence saddens all the grove.

Unhappy

Unhappy Italy! whose alter'd state
Has felt the worst severity of fate:
Not that Barbarian hands her Fasces broke,
And bow'd her haughty neck beneath their yoke;
Not that her palaces to earth are thrown,
Her cities desert, and her fields unsown;
But that her ancient Spirit is decay'd,
That sacred Wisdom from her bounds is fled,
That there the source of Science flows no more,
Whence its rich streams supply'd the world before.

Illustrious names; that once in Latium shin'd,
Born to instruct and to command mankind;
Chiefs, by whose virtue mighty Rome was rais'd,
And Poets, who those Chiefs sublimely prais'd;
Oft I the traces you have left explore,
Your ashes visit, and your urns adore;
Oft kiss, with lips devout, some mould'ring stone,
With ivy's venerable shade o'ergrown;
Those hallow'd ruins better pleas'd to see
Than all the pomp of modern luxury.

As late on Virgil's tomb fresh flow'rs I strow'd,
While with th' inspiring Muse my bosom glow'd,
Crown'd with eternal bays my ravish'd eyes
Beheld the poet's awful form arise;
Stranger, he said, whose pious hand has paid
These grateful rites to my attentive shade,
When thou shalt breathe thy happy native air,
To Pope this message from his Master bear:

' Great

' Great Bard, whose numbers I myself inspire,
To whom I gave my own harmonious lyre,
If high-exalted on the throne of Wit,
Near me and Homer thou aspire to sit,
No more let meaner Satire dim the rays
That flow majestic from thy nobler bays.
In all the flow'ry paths of Pindus stray,
But shun that thorny, that unpleasing way;
Nor when each soft engaging Muse is thine,
Address the least attractive of the Nine.
 Of thee more worthy were the task, to raise
A lasting column to thy Country's praise;
To sing the land, which yet alone can boast
That Liberty corrupted Rome has lost;
Where Science in the arms of Peace is laid,
And plants her Palm beside the Olive's shade.
Such was the theme for which my lyre I strung,
Such was the people whose exploits I sung;
Brave, yet refin'd, for arms and arts renown'd,
With diff'rent bays by Mars and Phœbus crown'd;
Dauntless opposers of tyrannic sway,
But pleas'd a mild Augustus to obey.
 If these commands submissive thou receive,
Immortal and unblam'd thy name shall live;
Envy to black Cocytus shall retire,
And howl with Furies in tormenting fire;
Approving Time shall consecrate thy lays,
And join the Patriot's to the Poet's praise.'

To

To my LORD HERVEY.

In the Year 1730.

From WORCESTERSHIRE. By the Same.

Strenua nos exercet Inertia: Navibus atque
Quadrigis petimus bene Vivere: quod petis hic est;
Est Ulubris, Animus si te non deficit æquus.
                                                    HOR.

FAV'RITE of Venus and the tuneful Nine,
  Pollio, by nature form'd in courts to shine,
Wilt thou once more a kind attention lend
To thy long absent and forgotten friend:
Who after seas and mountains wander'd o'er,
Return'd at length to his own native shore,
From all that's gay retir'd, and all that's great,
Beneath the shades of his paternal seat
Has found that happiness he sought in vain
On the fam'd banks of Tiber and of Seine?
  'Tis not to view the well-proportion'd pile,
The charms of Titian's and of Raphael's stile;
At soft Italian sounds to melt away;
Or in the fragrant groves of myrtle stray;

That lulls the tumults of the soul to rest,
Or makes the fond possessor truly blest.
In our own breasts the source of Pleasure lies
Still open, and still flowing to the wise;
Not forc'd by toilsome art and wild desire
Beyond the bounds of nature to aspire,
But in its proper channels gliding fair;
A common benefit, which all may share.
Yet half mankind this easy good disdain,
Nor relish happiness unbought by pain;
False is their taste of bliss, and thence their search is vain.
So idle, yet so restless are our minds,
We climb the Alps, and brave the raging winds,
Through various toils to seek content we roam,
Which with but *thinking right* were our's at home:
For not the ceaseless change of shifted place
Can from the heart a settled grief erase:
Nor can the purer balm of foreign air
Heal the distemper'd mind of aching care.
The wretch by wild impatience driv'n to rove,
Vex'd with the pangs of ill-requited love,
From pole to pole the fatal arrow bears,
Whose rooted point his bleeding bosom tears,
With equal pain each diff'rent clime he tries,
And is himself that torment which he flies.

   For how should ills, that from our passions flow,
Be chang'd by Afric's heat, or Russia's snow?

Or how can aught but pow'rful Reason cure,
What from unthinking Folly we endure?
Happy is He, and He alone, who knows
His heart's uneasy discord to compose;
In gen'rous love of others' good to find
The sweetest pleasures of the social mind;
To bound his wishes in their proper sphere;
To nourish pleasing hope, and conquer anxious fear.
This was the wisdom ancient Sages taught,
This was the sov'reign good they justly sought;
This to no place or climate is confin'd,
But the free native produce of the mind.

   Nor think, my Lord, that Courts to you deny
The useful practice of Philosophy:
Horace, the wisest of the tuneful choir,
Not always chose from Greatness to retire,
But in the palace of Augustus knew
The same unerring maxims to pursue,
Which in the Sabine or the Velian shade
His study and his happiness he made.

   May you, my friend, by his example taught,
View all the giddy scene with sober thought;
Undazzled every glittering folly see,
And in the midst of slavish forms be free;
In its own center keep your steady mind;
Let Prudence guide you, but let Honour bind;
In show, in manners, act the Courtier's part,
But be a Country-gentleman at heart.

ADVICE to a LADY.

By the Same. 1731.

THE counsels of a friend, Belinda, hear,
Too roughly kind to please a Lady's ear,
Unlike the flatt'ries of a lover's pen,
Such truths as women seldom learn from men.
Nor think I praise you ill, when thus I shew
What female Vanity might fear to know:
Some merit's mine, to dare to be sincere,
But greater your's, sincerity to bear.

Hard is the fortune that your sex attends;
Women, like Princes, find few real friends:
All who approach them their own ends pursue:
Lovers and ministers are seldom true.
Hence oft from Reason heedless Beauty strays,
And the most trusted Guide the most betrays:
Hence by fond dreams of fancy'd pow'r amus'd,
When most you tyrannize you're most abus'd.

What is your sex's earliest, latest care,
Your heart's supreme ambition? To be fair:
For this the toilet every thought employs,
Hence all the toils of dress, and all the joys:

For

For this, hands, lips, and eyes are put to school,
And each inftructed feature has its rule;
And yet how few have learnt, when this is giv'n,
Not to difgrace the partial boon of heav'n?
How few with all their pride of form can move?
How few are lovely, that were made for love?
Do you, my fair, endeavour to poffefs
An elegance of mind as well as drefs;
Be that your ornament, and know to pleafe
By graceful Nature's unaffected eafe.

 Nor make to dang'rous Wit a vain pretence,
But wifely reft content with modeft Senfe;
For Wit, like wine, intoxicates the brain,
Too ftrong for feeble woman to fuftain;
Of thofe who claim it, more than half have none,
And half of thofe who have it, are undone.

 Be ftill fuperior to your fex's arts,
Nor think Difhonefty a proof of Parts;
For you the plaineft is the wifeft rule,
A Cunning Woman is a Knavish Fool.

 Be good yourfelf, nor think another's fhame
Can raife your merit, or adorn your fame.
Prudes rail at whores, as ftatefmen in difgrace
At minifters, becaufe they wifh their place.
Virtue is amiable, mild, ferene,
Without, all beauty, and all peace within:
The honour of a prude is rage and ftorm,
'Tis uglinefs in its moft frightful form:

Fiercely

Fiercely it stands defying gods and men,
As fiery monsters guard a giant's den.
   Seek to be good, but aim not to be great:
A woman's noblest station is Retreat;
Her fairest virtues fly from public sight,
Domestic worth, that shuns too strong a light.
   To rougher man Ambition's task resign:
'Tis ours in Senates or in Courts to shine,
To labour for a sunk corrupted state,
Or dare the rage of envy, and be great.
One only care your gentle breasts should move,
Th' important business of your life is Love:
To this great point direct your constant aim,
This makes your Happiness, and this your Fame.
   Be never cool reserve with passion join'd;
With caution chuse; but then be fondly kind.
The selfish heart, that but by halves is giv'n,
Shall find no place in Love's delightful heav'n;
Here sweet extremes alone can truly bless;
The virtue of a lover is excess.
   A maid unask'd may own a well-plac'd flame,
Not loving *first*, but loving *wrong* is shame.
   Contemn the little pride of giving pain,
Nor think that conquest justifies disdain;
Short is the period of insulting Pow'r;
Offended Cupid finds his vengeful hour,
Soon will resume the empire which he gave,
And soon the Tyrant shall become the Slave.

                                          Blest

Bleſt is the maid, and worthy to be bleſt,
Whoſe ſoul, entire by him ſhe loves poſſeſs'd,
Feels every vanity in fondneſs loſt,
And aſks no pow'r, but that of pleaſing moſt:
Her's is the bliſs in juſt return to prove
The honeſt warmth of undiſſembled Love;
For her, inconſtant man might ceaſe to range,
And Gratitude forbid Deſire to change.

But leſt harſh Care the lover's peace deſtroy,
And roughly blight the tender buds of joy,
Let Reaſon teach what Paſſion fain would hide,
That Hymen's bands by Prudence ſhould be ty'd.
Venus in vain the wedded pair would crown,
If angry Fortune on their union frown:
Soon will the flatt'ring dream of bliſs be o'er,
And cloy'd imagination cheat no more.
Then waking to the ſenſe of laſting pain,
With mutual tears the nuptial couch they ſtain;
And that fond love, which ſhould afford relief,
Does but increaſe the anguiſh of their grief;
While both could eaſier their own ſorrows bear,
Than the ſad knowledge of each other's care.

Yet may you rather feel that virtuous pain,
Than ſell your violated charms for gain;
Than wed the wretch whom you deſpiſe, or hate,
For the vain glare of uſeleſs wealth or ſtate.
The moſt abandon'd proſtitutes are they,
Who not to Love, but Av'rice fall a prey:

Nor aught avails the specious name of WIFE;
A maid so wedded is a WHORE FOR LIFE.

 Ev'n in the happiest choice, where fav'ring Heav'n
Has equal love, and easy fortune giv'n,
Think not, the Husband gain'd, that all is done;
The prize of happiness must still be won;
And oft, the careless find it to their cost,
The *Lover* in the *Husband* may be lost;
The *Graces* might *alone* his heart *allure*;
They and the *Virtues meeting* must *secure*.

 Let ev'n your *Prudence* wear the pleasing dress
Of care for *him*, and anxious *tenderness*.
From kind concern about his weal or woe,
Let each domestic duty seem to flow;
The HOUSHOLD SCEPTER if he bids you bear,
Make it your pride his *servant* to appear;
Endearing thus the common acts of life,
The *Mistress* still shall charm him in the *Wife*;
And wrinkled age shall unobserv'd come on,
Before his eye perceives one beauty gone;
Ev'n o'er your cold, and ever-sacred urn,
His constant flame shall unextinguish'd burn.

 Thus I, Belinda, would your charms improve,
And form your heart to all the arts of Love;
The task were harder to secure my own
Against the pow'r of those already known;
For well you twist the secret chains that bind
With gentle force the captivated mind.

          Skill'd

Skill'd every soft attraction to employ,
Each flatt'ring hope, and each alluring joy:
I own your genius, and from you receive
The rules of Pleasing, which to you I give.

SONG.

Written in the Year 1732. By the Same.

I.

WHEN Delia on the plain appears,
  Aw'd by a thousand tender fears,
I would approach, but dare not move;—
Tell me, my Heart, if this be Love.

II.

Whene'er she speaks, my ravish'd ear
No other voice but her's can hear,
No other wit but her's approve;—
Tell me, my Heart, if this be Love.

III.

If she some other youth commend,
Though I was once his fondest friend,
His instant enemy I prove;—
Tell me, my Heart, if this be Love.

IV. When

IV.

When she is absent, I no more
Delight in all that pleas'd before,
The clearest spring, or shadiest grove;—
Tell me, my Heart, if this be Love.

V.

When fond of pow'r, of beauty vain,
Her nets she spread for every swain,
I strove to hate, but vainly strove;—
Tell me, my Heart, if this be Love.

SONG.

Written in the Year 1733. By the Same.

I.

THE heavy hours are almost past
  That part my Love and me;
My longing eyes may hope at last,
  Their only wish to see.

II.

But how, my Delia, will you meet
  The man you've lost so long?
Will Love in all your pulses beat,
  And tremble on your tongue?

III.

Will you in every look declare
   Your heart is still the same?
And heal each idly anxious care
   Our fears in absence frame?

IV.

Thus, Delia, thus I paint the scene,
   When shortly we shall meet,
And try what yet remains between
   Of loit'ring time to cheat.

V.

But if the dream that sooths my mind
   Shall false and groundless prove;
If I am doom'd at length to find
   You have forgot to love;

VI.

All I of Venus ask, is this;
   No more to let us join;
But grant me here the flatt'ring bliss,
   To die and think you mine.

DAMON

DAMON and DELIA.

In Imitation of HORACE and LYDIA.

Written in the Year 1732. By the Same.

DAMON.

TELL me, my Delia, tell me why
My kindeſt, fondeſt looks you fly:
What means this cloud upon your brow?
Have I offended? tell me how?
Some change has happen'd in your heart,
Some rival there has ſtol'n a part;
Reaſon theſe fears may diſapprove:
But yet I fear, becauſe I love.

DELIA.

First, tell me, Damon, why to-day
At Belvidera's feet you lay?
Why with ſuch warmth her charms you prais'd,
And ev'ry trifling beauty rais'd,
As if you meant to let me ſee
Your flatt'ry is not All for me?
Alas! too well your ſex I knew,
Nor was ſo weak to think you true.

DAMON.

Damon.

Unkind! my falsehood to upbraid
When your own orders I obey'd;
You bid me try by this deceit.
The notice of the world to cheat,
And hide beneath another name
The secret of our mutual flame.

Delia.

Damon, your prudence I confess,
But let me wish it had been less;
Too well the lover's part you play'd,
With too much art your court you made;
Had it been only art, your eyes
Would not have join'd in the disguise.

Damon.

Ah, cease thus idly to molest
With groundless fears thy virgin breast.
While thus at fancy'd wrongs you grieve,
To me a real pain you give.

Delia.

Though well I might your truth distrust,
My foolish heart believes you just;
Reason this faith may disapprove,
But I believe, because I love.

ODE, in Imitation of PASTOR FIDO.

(O Primavera Gioventu del Anno.)

Written Abroad in 1729. By the Same.

I.

PArent of blooming flow'rs and gay desires,
   Youth of the tender year, delightful Spring,
At whose approach, inspir'd with equal fires,
   The am'rous Nightingale and Poet sing:

II.

Again dost thou return, but not with thee
   Return the smiling hours I once possess'd;
Blessings thou bring'st to others, but to me
   The sad remembrance, that I once was bless'd.

III.

Thy faded charms, which Winter snatch'd away,
   Renew'd in all their former lustre shine;
But ah! no more shall hapless I be gay,
   Or know the vernal joys that have been mine.

IV.

Though linnets sing, though flow'rs adorn the green,
   Though on their wings soft zephyrs fragrance bear;
Harsh is the music, joyless is the scene,
   The odour faint; for Delia is not there.

V.

Cheerless and cold I feel the genial sun,
  From thee while absent I in exile rove;
Thy lovely presence, fairest light, alone!
  Can warm my heart to gladness and to love.

Part of an ELEGY of TIBULLUS, translated.

(Divitias alius fulvo sibi congerat Auro.)

1729-30. By the Same.

LET others heap of wealth a shining store,
  And much possessing, labour still for more;
Let them, disquieted with dire alarms,
Aspire to win a dangerous fame in arms:
Me tranquil poverty shall lull to rest,
Humbly secure and indolently blest;
Warm'd by the blaze of my own chearful hearth,
I'll waste the wintry hours in social mirth;
In summer pleas'd attend to harvest toils,
In autumn press the vineyard's purple spoils,
And oft to Delia in my bosom bear
Some kid, or lamb that wants its mother's care:
With her I'll celebrate each gladsome day,
When swains their sportive rites to Bacchus pay:

With her new milk on Pales' altar pour,
And deck with ripen'd fruits Pomona's bow'r.
At night how soothing would it be to hear,
Shelter'd and warm, the tempest whistling near;
And while my charmer in my arms I strain,
Slumber assisted by the beating rain!
Ah! how much happier, than the fool who braves
In search of wealth the black tempestuous waves!
While I, contented with my little store,
In tedious voyage seek no distant shore,
But idly lolling on some shady seat,
Near cooling fountains shun the dog-star's heat;
For what reward so rich could Fortune give
That I by absence should my Delia grieve?
Let great Messalla shine in martial toils,
And grace his palace with triumphal spoils;
Me Beauty holds in strong, though gentle chains,
Far from tumultuous war, and dusty plains.
With thee, my love, to pass my tranquil days,
How would I slight ambition's painful praise!
How would I joy with thee, my love, to yoke
The ox, and feed my solitary flock!
On thy soft breast might I but lean my head,
How downy should I think the woodland bed!

 The wretch who sleeps not by his fair one's side,
Detests the gilded couch's useless pride,
Nor knows his weary, weeping eyes to close,
Though murm'ring rills invite him to repose.

Hard

Hard was his heart, who thee, my fair, could leave
For all the honours profp'rous War can give;
Though through the vanquifh'd eaft he fpread his fame,
And Parthian tyrants trembled at his name;
Though bright in arms, while hofts around him bleed,
With martial pride he prefs'd his foaming fteed.
No pomps like thefe my humble vows require;
I afk, in thy embraces to expire:
Thee may my clofing eyes in death behold!
Thee may my fault'ring hand yet ftrive to hold!
Then, Delia, then thy heart will melt in woe,
Then o'er my breathlefs clay thy tears will flow;
Thy tears will flow, for gentle is thy mind,
Nor doft thou think it weaknefs to be kind.
With thee each youth and tender maid fhall join
In grief, and mix their friendly fighs with thine:
But ah! my Delia, I conjure thee, fpare
Thy heaving breafts and loofe difhevell'd hair:
Wound not thy form; left on th' Elyfian coaft
Thy anguifh fhould difturb my peaceful ghoft.

 But now nor death, nor parting fhould employ
Our fprightly thoughts, or damp our bridal joy:
We'll live, my Delia, and from life remove
All care, all bus'nefs, but delightful Love.
Old-age in vain thofe pleafures would retrieve,
Which youth alone can tafte, alone can give;
Then let us fnatch the moment to be bleft,
This hour is Love's—be Fortune's all the reft.

         SONG.

SONG.

Written in the Year 1732. By the Same.

I.

SAY, Myra, why is gentle Love
   A stranger to that mind,
Which pity and esteem can move;
   Which can be just and kind?

II.

Is it because you fear to share
   The ills that Love molest:
The jealous Doubt, the tender Care,
   That rack the am'rous breast?

III.

Alas! by some degree of woe
   We every bliss must gain:
The heart can ne'er a transport know,
   That never feels a pain.

Written at Mr. POPE's House at Twickenham, which he had lent to Mrs. Grenville [a].

In AUGUST 1735. By the Same.

I.

GO, Thames, and tell the busy town,
  Not all its wealth or pride
Could tempt me from the charms that crown
  Thy rural flow'ry side:

II.

Thy flow'ry side, where POPE has plac'd
  The Muses' green retreat,
With ev'ry smile of Nature grac'd,
  With every Art compleat.

III.

But now, sweet bard, thy heav'nly song
  Enchants us here no more;
Their darling glory lost too long
  Thy once-lov'd shades deplore.

---

[a] The author's aunt, afterwards created countess Temple. She was widow and relict of Richard Grenville of Wootton, Esq; and died October 6, 1752.

IV.

Yet ſtill for beauteous Grenville's ſake,
  The Muſes here remain;
Grenville, whoſe eyes have power to make
  A POPE of every ſwain.

EPIGRAM.

By the Same.

NONE without Hope e'er lov'd the brighteſt Fair,
  But Love can hope where Reaſon would deſpair.

To Mr. WEST[a], at Wickham[b].

Written in the Year 1740.

By the Same.

FAIR Nature's sweet simplicity
   With elegance refin'd,
Well in thy Seat, my friend, I see,
   But better in thy Mind.
To both from courts and all their state
   Eager I fly, to prove
Joys far above a courtier's fate,
   Tranquillity and love.

---

[a] Gilbert West, Esq; the author's cousin.   [b] Near Croyden.

To Miss LUCY FORTESCUE [a].

By the Same.

ONCE by the Muse alone inspir'd
   I sung my am'rous strains:
No serious love my bosom fir'd;
Yet every tender maid, deceiv'd,
The idly mournful tale believ'd,
   And wept my fancy'd pains.

But Venus now to punish me,
   For having feign'd so well,
Has made my heart so fond of thee,
That not the whole Aonian quire
Can accents soft enough inspire,
   Its real flame to tell.

---

[a] The authors' first lady, whose death, which happened 19th January 1746-7, he so pathetically lamented in the Monody printed in this volume.

To the Same, with HAMMOND's Elegies.

ALL that of Love can be express'd
  In these soft numbers see;
But, LUCY, would you know the rest,
  It must be read in me.

To the Same.

TO him who in an hour must die,
  Not swifter seems that hour to fly,
Than slow the minutes seem to me,
Which keep me from the sight of thee.

Not more that trembling wretch would give
Another day or year to live;
Than I to shorten what remains
Of that long hour which thee detains.

Oh! come to my impatient arms,
Oh! come with all thy heav'nly charms,
At once to justify and pay
The pain I feel from this delay.

To the Same.

I.

TO ease my troubled mind of anxious care,
  Last night the secret casket I explor'd;
Where all the letters of my absent fair,
  (His richest treasure) careful Love had stor'd:

II.

In every word a magic spell I found
  Of pow'r to charm each busy thought to rest,
Though every word increas'd the tender wound
  Of fond desire still throbbing in my breast.

III.

So to his hoarded gold the miser steals,
  And loses every sorrow at the sight;
Yet wishes still for more, nor ever feels
  Entire contentment, or secure delight.

IV.

Ah! should I lose thee, my too lovely maid,
  Couldst thou forget thy heart was ever mine,
Fear not thy letters should the change upbraid:
  My hand each dear memorial shall resign:

V.

Not one kind word shall in my pow'r remain
  A painful witness of reproach to thee:
And lest my heart should still their sense retain,
  My heart shall break, to leave thee wholly free.

A Prayer

A Prayer to Venus, in her Temple at Stowe.

To the Same.

I.

FAIR Venus, whose delightful shrine surveys
 Its front reflected in the silver lake,
These humble off'rings, which thy servant pays,
 Fresh flowers, and myrtle wreaths, propitious take.

II.

If less my love exceeds all other love,
 Than Lucy's charms all other charms excel,
Far from my breast each soothing hope remove,
 And there let sad despair for ever dwell.

III.

But if my soul is fill'd with her alone,
 No other wish, nor other object knows,
Oh! make her, Goddess, make her all my own,
 And give my trembling heart secure repose.

IV.

No watchful spies I ask to guard her charms,
 No walls of brass, no steel-defended door;
Place her but once within my circling arms,
 Love's surest fort, and I will doubt no more.

To the Same.

On her pleading want of TIME.

I.

ON Thames's bank, a gentle youth
For LUCY sigh'd with matchless truth,
    Ev'n when he sigh'd in rhyme;
The lovely maid his flame return'd,
And would with equal warmth have burn'd
    But that she had not Time.

II.

Oft he repair'd with eager feet
In secret shades his fair to meet
    Beneath th' accustom'd lyme;
She would have fondly met him there,
And heal'd with love each tender care,
    But that she had not Time.

III.

" It was not thus, inconstant maid,
" You acted once (the shepherd said)
    " When love was in its prime:"
She griev'd to hear him thus complain,
And would have writ to ease his pain,
    But that she had not Time.

IV.

How can you act so cold a part?
No crime of mine has chang'd your heart,
    If Love be not a crime.———
We soon must part for months, for years———
She would have answer'd with her tears,
    But that she had not Time.

To the Same.

YOUR shape, your lips, your eyes are still the same,
    Still the bright object of my constant flame;
But where is now the tender glance, that stole
With gentle sweetness my enchanted soul?
Kind fears, impatient wishes, soft desires,
Each melting charm that love alone inspires.
These, these are lost; and I behold no more
The maid, my heart delighted to adore.
Yet still unchang'd, still doating to excess,
I ought, but dare not, try to love you less;
Weakly I grieve, unpity'd I complain;
But not unpunish'd shall your change remain;
For you, cold maid, whom no complaints can move,
Were far more blest, when you like me could love.

To the Same.

I.
WHEN I think on your truth, I doubt you no more,
I blame all the fears I gave way to before,
I say to my heart, "Be at rest, and believe
"That whom once she has chosen she never will leave."

II.
But ah! when I think on each ravishing grace
That plays in the smiles of that heavenly face,
My heart beats again; I again apprehend
Some fortunate rival in every friend.

III.
These painful suspicions you cannot remove,
Since you neither can lessen your charms nor my love;
But doubts caus'd by passion you never can blame;
For they are not ill founded, or you feel the same.

To the Same with a NEW WATCH.

WITH me while present, may thy lovely eyes
    Be never turn'd upon this golden toy:
Think every pleasing hour too swiftly flies,
    And measure time, by joy succeeding joy.

But when the cares that interrupt our bliss
    To me not always will thy sight allow,
Then oft with kind impatience look on this,
    Then every minute count—as I do now.

An Irregular ODE,

Written at Wickham in 1746.

To the Same.

I.

YE sylvan scenes with artless beauty gay,
    Ye gentle shades of Wickham, say,
What is the charm that each successive year,
    Which sees me with my LUCY here,
   Can thus to my transported heart
A sense of joy unfelt before impart?

II.

Is it glad Summer's balmy breath that blows
From the fair jess'mine, and the blushing rose?
Her balmy breath, and all her blooming store
    Of rural bliss was here before:
Oft have I met her on the verdant side
Of Norwood-hill, and in the yellow meads,
    Where Pan the dancing Graces leads,
    Array'd in all her flow'ry pride.
No sweeter fragrance now the gardens yield,
No brighter colours paint th' enamel'd field.

III.

Is it to Love thefe new delights I owe?
    Four times has the revolving fun
His annual circle through the zodiac run;
    Since all that Love's indulgent pow'r
    On favour'd mortals can beftow,
Was giv'n to me in this aufpicious bow'r.

IV.

Here firft my LUCY, fweet in virgin charms,
    Was yielded to my longing arms;
    And round our nuptial bed,
Hov'ring with purple wings, th' Idalian boy
Shook from his radiant torch the blifsful fires
    Of innocent defires,
While Venus fcatter'd myrtles o'er her head.
    Whence then this ftrange increafe of joy?
He, only he can tell, who match'd like me,
(If fuch another happy man there be)
    Has by his own experience try'd
How much *the Wife* is dearer than *the Bride*.

To the MEMORY of the same LADY.
A MONODY. A.D. 1747.

Ipse cavâ solans ægrum testudine amorem,
Te dulcis conjux, te solo in littore secum,
Te veniente die, te decedente canebat.

By the Same.

I.

AT length escap'd from every human eye,
    From every duty, every care,
That in my mournful thoughts might claim a share,
Or force my tears their flowing stream to dry,
Beneath the gloom of this embow'ring shade,
This lone retreat, for tender sorrow made,
I now may give my burden'd heart relief,
    And pour forth all my stores of grief,
Of grief surpassing every other woe,
Far as the purest bliss, the happiest love
    Can on th' ennobled mind bestow,
Exceeds the vulgar joys that move
Our gross desires, inelegant and low.

II.

Ye tufted groves, ye gently-falling rills,
    Ye high o'ershadowing hills,
Ye lawns gay-smiling with eternal green,
    Oft have you my LUCY seen!

But never shall you now behold her more:
    Nor will she now with fond delight
And taste refin'd your rural charms explore.
Clos'd are those beauteous eyes in endless night,
Those beauteous eyes where beaming us'd to shine
Reason's pure light, and Virtue's spark divine.

III.

Oft would the Dryads of these woods rejoice
    To hear her heav'nly voice,
For her despising, when she deign'd to sing,
    The sweetest songsters of the spring:
The woodlark and the linnet pleas'd no more;
    The nightingale was mute,
    And every shepherd's flute
    Was cast in silent scorn away,
While all attended to her sweeter lay.
Ye larks and linnets now resume your song,
    And thou, melodious Philomel,
    Again thy plaintive story tell,
For death has stop'd that tuneful tongue,
Whose music could alone your warbling notes excel.

IV.

    In vain I look around,
    O'er all the well-known ground,
My Lucy's wonted footsteps to descry;
    Where oft we us'd to walk,
    Where oft in tender talk
We saw the summer sun go down the sky;

Nor by yon fountain's side,
Nor where its waters glide
Along the valley, can she now be found:
In all the wide-stretch'd prospect's ample bound
No more my mournful eye
Can aught of her espy,
But the sad secret earth where her dear relics lie.

V.

O shades of Hagley, where is now your boast?
Your bright inhabitant is lost.
You she preferr'd to all the gay resorts
Where female vanity might wish to shine,
The pomp of cities, and the pride of courts.
Her modest beauties shun'd the public eye;
To your sequester'd dales
And flow'r-embroider'd vales
From an admiring world she chose to fly;
With Nature there retir'd, and Nature's GOD,
The silent paths of wisdom trod,
And banish'd every passion from her breast,
But those, the gentlest and the best,
Whose holy flames with energy divine
The virtuous heart enliven and improve,
The conjugal, and the maternal love.

VI.

Sweet babes, who, like the little playful fawns,
Were wont to trip along these verdant lawns

    By your delighted Mother's fide,
    Who now your infant steps shall guide?
Ah! where is now the hand whose tender care
To every Virtue would have form'd your Youth,
And strew'd with flow'rs the thorny ways of Truth?
        O loss beyond repair!
        O wretched Father left alone
To weep their dire misfortune, and thy own!
How shall thy weaken'd mind, oppress'd with woe,
    And drooping o'er thy Lucy's grave,
Perform the duties that you doubly owe,
        Now she, alas! is gone,
From folly, and from vice, their helpless age to save?

VII.

Where were ye, Muses, when relentless Fate
From these fond arms your fair disciple tore,
    From these fond arms that vainly strove
    With hapless ineffectual Love
To guard her bosom from the mortal blow?
    Could not your fav'ring pow'r, Aonian maids,
Could not, alas! your pow'r prolong her date,
    For whom so oft in these inspiring shades,
Or under Campden's moss-clad mountains hoar,
    You open'd all your sacred store,
    Whate'er your ancient sages taught,
    Your ancient bards sublimely thought,
And bade her raptur'd breast with all your spirit glow?

VIII.

Nor then did Pindus' or Castalia's plain,
Or Aganippe's fount your steps detain,
Nor in the Thespian vallies did you play;
 Nor then on [a] Mincio's bank
 Beset with osiers dank,
Nor where [b] Clitumnus rolls his gentle stream,
 Nor where through hanging woods
 Steep [c] Anio pours his floods;
Nor yet where [d] Meles, or [e] Ilissus stray.
 Ill does it now beseem,
 That, of your guardian care bereft,
To dire disease and death your darling should be left

IX.

Now what avails it that in early bloom,
 When light fantastic toys
 Are all her sex's joys,
With you she search'd the wit of Greece and Rome?
 And all that in her latter days
 To emulate her ancient praise

---

[a] The Mincio runs by Mantua, the birth-place of VIRGIL.

[b] The Clitumnus is a river of Umbria, the residence of PROPERTIUS.

[c] The Anio runs through Tiber or Tivoli, where HORACE had a villa.

[d] The Meles is a river of Ionia, from whence HOMER, supposed to be born on its banks, is called Melisigenes.

[e] The Ilissus is a river at Athens.

Italia's happy genius could produce;
    Or what the Gallic fire
    Bright-sparkling could inspire;
By all the Graces temper'd and refin'd;
    Or what in Britain's isle,
    Most favour'd with your smile,
The pow'rs of reason and of fancy join'd
To full perfection have conspir'd to raise?
    Ah! what is now the use
Of all these treasures that enrich'd her mind;
To black oblivion's gloom for ever now consign'd?

X.

    At least, ye Nine, her spotless name
    'Tis yours from death to save,
And in the temple of immortal Fame
With golden characters her worth engrave.
    Come then, ye virgin sisters, come,
And strew with choicest flow'rs her hallow'd tomb.
But foremost thou, in sable vestment clad,
    With accents sweet and sad,
Thou, plaintive Muse, whom o'er his Laura's urn
    Unhappy Petrarch call'd to mourn,
O come, and to this fairer Laura pay
A more impassion'd tear, a more pathetic lay.

XI.

Tell how each beauty of her mind and face
Was brighten'd by some sweet, peculiar grace!
    How eloquent in every look
Through her expressive eyes her soul distinctly spoke!

Tell how her manners by the world refin'd
Left all the taint of modish vice behind,
And made each charm of polish'd courts agree
   With candid Truth's simplicity,
   And uncorrupted Innocence!
   Tell how to more than manly sense
   She join'd the soft'ning influence
   Of more than female tenderness:
How in the thoughtless days of wealth and joy,
Which oft the care of others' good destroy,
    Her kindly-melting heart,
   To every want and every woe,
   To guilt itself when in distress,
   The balm of pity would impart,
And all relief that bounty could bestow!
Ev'n for the kid or lamb that pour'd its life
    Beneath the bloody knife,
    Her gentle tears would fall,
Tears from sweet Virtue's source, benevolent to all.

XII.

   Not only good and kind,
But strong and elevated was her mind:
   A spirit that with noble pride
    Could look superior down
    On Fortune's smile or frown;
   That could without regret or pain
To Virtue's lowest duty sacrifice
Or int'rest or ambition's highest prize:
That injur'd or offended never try'd

Its dignity by vengeance to maintain,
　　But by magnanimous difdain.
　A wit that temperately bright,
　　　With inoffenfive light
　All pleafing fhone, nor ever paft
The decent bounds that Wifdom's fober hand,
And fweet Benevolence's mild command,
And bafhful Modefty before it caft.
A prudence undeceiving, undeceiv'd,
That nor too little, nor too much believ'd,
That fcorn'd unjuft Sufpicion's coward fear,
And without weaknefs knew to be fincere.
Such LUCY was, when in her faireft days,
Amidft th' acclaim of univerfal praife,
　In life's and glory's frefheft bloom
Death came remorfelefs on, and funk her to the tomb.

XIII.

So where the filent ftreams of Liris glide,
In the foft bofom of Campania's vale,
When now the wintry tempefts all are fled,
And genial Summer breathes her gentle gale,
The verdant orange lifts its beauteous head:
From ev'ry branch the balmy flow'rets rife,
On every bough the golden fruits are feen;
With odours fweet it fills the fmiling fkies,
The wood-nymphs tend it, and th' Idalian queen:
But in the midft of all its blooming pride

VOL. II.　　　　　　F　　　　　A fudden

A sudden blaft from Apenninus blows,
    Cold with perpetual snows :
The tender blighted plant shrinks up its leaves, and dies.

XIV.

Arise, O Petrarch, from th' Elysian bow'rs,
    With never-fading myrtles twin'd,
    And fragrant with ambrosial flowers,
Where to thy Laura thou again art join'd;
Arise, and hither bring the silver lyre,
    Tun'd by thy skilful hand,
To the soft notes of elegant desire,
    With which o'er many a land
Was spread the fame of thy disastrous love;
    To me resign the vocal shell,
    And teach my sorrows to relate
    Their melancholy tale so well,
    As may ev'n things inanimate,
Rough mountain oaks, and desart rocks, to pity move.

XV.

What were, alas! thy woes compar'd to mine?
To thee thy mistress in the blissful band
    Of Hymen never gave her hand;
The joys of wedded love were never thine.
    In thy domestic care
    She never bore a share,
    Nor with endearing art
    Would heal thy wounded heart
Of every secret grief that fester'd there:

Nor did her fond affection on the bed
Of sickness watch thee, and thy languid head
Whole nights on her unwearied arm sustain,
    And charm away the sense of pain:
    Nor did she crown your mutual flame
With pledges dear, and with a father's tender name.

XVI.

O best of wives! O dearer far to me
    Than when thy virgin charms
    Were yielded to my arms,
How can my soul endure the loss of thee?
How in the world, to me a desart grown,
    Abandon'd, and alone,
Without my sweet companion can I live?
    Without thy lovely smile,
The dear reward of every virtuous toil,
What pleasures now can pall'd Ambition give?
Ev'n the delightful sense of well-earn'd praise,
Unshar'd by thee, no more my lifeless thoughts could raise.

XVII.

    For my distracted mind
    What succour can I find?
On whom for consolation shall I call?
    Support me, every friend,
    Your kind assistance lend
To bear the weight of this oppressive woe.
    Alas! each friend of mine,
My dear departed love, so much was thine,
That none has any comfort to bestow.

My books, the best relief
In every other grief,
Are now with your idea sadden'd all:
Each fav'rite author we together read
My tortur'd mem'ry wounds, and speaks of Lucy dead.

XVIII.

We were the happiest pair of human kind!
The rolling year its varying course perform'd,
And back return'd again;
Another and another smiling came,
And saw our happiness unchang'd remain;
Still in her golden chain
Harmonious Concord did our wishes bind:
Our studies, pleasures, taste, the same.
O fatal, fatal stroke,
That all this pleasing fabric Love had rais'd
Of rare felicity,
On which ev'n wanton Vice with envy gaz'd,
And every scheme of bliss our hearts had form'd
With soothing hope, for many a future day,
In one sad moment broke!
Yet, O my soul, thy rising murmurs stay,
Nor dare th' all-wise Disposer to arraign,
Or against his supreme decree
With impious grief complain.
That all thy full-blown joys at once should fade
Was his most righteous will, and be that will obey'd.

XIX. Would

XIX.

Would thy fond love his grace to her controul,
And in thefe low abodes of fin and pain
   Her pure, exalted foul
Unjuftly for thy partial good detain?
No—rather ftrive thy grov'ling mind to raife
   Up to that unclouded blaze,
That heav'nly radiance of eternal light,
In which enthron'd fhe now with pity fees
   How frail, how infecure, how flight,
     Is every mortal blifs;
Ev'n love itfelf, if rifing by degrees
Beyond the bounds of this imperfect ftate,
   Whofe fleeting joys fo foon muft end,
It does not to its fov'reign Good afcend.
   Rife then, my foul, with hope elate,
And feek thofe regions of ferene delight,
Whofe peaceful path and ever-open gate
No feet but thofe of harden'd Guilt fhall mifs.
   There Death himfelf thy Lucy fhall reftore,
There yield up all his pow'r e'er to divide you more.

AN EPITAPH[a].

By the Same.

To the
Memory of Lucy Lyttelton,
Daughter of Hugh Fortescue of Filleigh
in the County of Devon, Esq;
Father to the present Earl of Clinton,
By Lucy his wife,
The daughter of Matthew Lord Aylmer;
Who departed this life the 19th of Jan. 1746-7,
Aged twenty-nine,
Having employ'd the short term assign'd to her here,
In the uniform practice of Religion and Virtue.

MADE to engage all hearts, and charm all eyes;
    Tho' meek, magnanimous; tho' witty, wise;
Polite, as all her life in courts had been;
Yet good, as she the world had never seen;

[a] This Epitaph is inscribed on a monument erected in the church of Hagley. It consists of a beautiful urn, on a pedestal of the finest white marble; on the front of which is carved in relievo a female face in profile, and under it the word Luciæ. The figure of Hymen rests on the pedestal, with his torch extinct, weeping, and looking towards the urn. Besides the above inscription, there is another in Latin.

The noble fire of an exalted mind,
With gentle female tenderness combin'd.
Her Speech was the melodious voice of Love,
Her Song the warbling of the vernal Grove;
Her Eloquence was sweeter than her Song,
Soft as her Heart, and as her Reason strong;
Her Form each beauty of her mind express'd,
Her mind was Virtue by the Graces dress'd.

ON THE ABUSE of TRAVELLING.

A CANTO,

In IMITATION of SPENSER.

By GILBERT WEST, Esq;[a]

THE ARGUMENT.

Archimage tempts the Red-Cross Knight
From love of Fairy-land,
With show of foreign pleasures all,
The which he doth withstand.

I.

WISE was that Spartan Law-giver [b] of old,
   Who rais'd on Virtue's base his well-built state,
Exiling from her walls barbaric gold,
With all the mischiefs that upon it wait,
                                        Corruption,

---

[a] Gilbert West was the son of Dr. West, by a sister of Sir Richard Temple, afterwards Lord Cobham. He was educated at Eton and Oxford, but quitted an academical life by the recommendation of his uncle,

Corruption, luxury, and envious hate;
And the distinctions proud of rich and poor,
Which among brethren kindle foul debate,
And teach Ambition, that to Fame would soar,
To the false lure of wealth her stooping wing to low'r.

II.

Yet would Corruption soon have entrance found,
And all his boasted schemes eftsoon decay'd,
Had not he cast a pow'rful circle round,
Which to a distance the arch-felon fray'd,

---

who procured for him a commission in a troop of horse. He continued some time in the army, but finding himself more inclined to civil employment, he resigned his commission, and engaged in business under the Lord Townsend, then Secretary of State, with whom he attended the King to Hanover. In May 1729, he was nominated a Clerk Extraordinary of the Privy Council, and soon afterwards married. He then settled at Wickham, where he devoted himself to learning and to piety. On the 30th of March 1748, he was complimented by the University of Oxford with the degree of Doctor of Laws, by diploma, for his excellent book on the Resurrection. In 1752, he became one of the Clerks of the Privy Council, and his friend Mr. Pitt about the same time made him Treasurer of Chelsea Hospital. He did not long enjoy these posts. In 1755, he lost his only son, and the year after, March 26, a stroke of the palsy, says Dr. Johnson, "brought to the "grave one of the few Poets, to whom the grave needed not to be "terrible."

b Lycurgus.

And

And ineffectual his foul engines made:
This was, to weet, that politic command,
Which from vain travel the young Spartan stay'd,
Ne suffer'd him forsake his native land,
To learn deceitful arts, and science contraband.

III.

Yet had the ancient world her courts and schools;
Great Kings and Courtiers civil and refin'd;
Great Rabbins, deeply read in Wisdom's rules,
And all the arts that cultivate the mind,
Embellish life, and polish human kind.
Such, Asia, birth-place of proud monarchy,
Such, elder Ægypt, in thy kingdoms shin'd,
Mysterious Egypt, the rank nursery
Of superstitions fond, and learned vanity.

IV.

But what accomplishments, what arts polite,
Did the young Spartan want his deeds to grace,
Whose manly virtues, and heroic spright,
Check'd by no thought impure, no falsehood base,
With nat'ral dignity might well outface
The glare of manners false, and mimic pride?
And wherefore should they range from place to place,
Who to their country's love so firm were ty'd,
All homely as she was, that for her oft they dy'd?

V.

And ^c sooth it is (with rev'rence may ye hear,
And honour due to passion so refin'd)
The strong affection which true patriots bear
To their dear country, zealous is and blind,
And fond as is the love of womankind,
So that they may not her defects espy,
Ne other ^d paragone may ever find,
But gazing on her with an aweful eye
And superstitious zeal, her learn to deify.

VI.

And, like as is the faith unsound, untrue,
Of him, who wand'ring aye from fair to fair,
Conceiveth from each object passion new,
Or from his heart quite drives the troublous care;
So with the patriot-lover doth it fare,
Who through the world delighting aye to rove,
His country changeth with each change of air,
Or weening the delights of all to prove,
On none, or all alike, bestows his vagrant love.

VII.

^e Als doth Corruption in a distant soil,
With double force ^f assay the youthful heart,
Expos'd suspectless to the traytor's wile,
Expos'd unwarn'd to Pleasure's poison'd dart,

---

^c truth. ^d rival, or one to compare with her.
^e moreover, besides. ^f assault.

Expos'd

Expos'd unpractis'd in the world's wide mart,
Where each one lies, imposes, and betrays,
Without a friend due counsel to impart,
Without a parent's awe to rule his ways,
Without the check of shame, or spur of public praise.

VIII.

[g] Forthy, false Archimago, traytor vile,
Who burnt 'gainst Fairy-land with ceaseless ire,
'Gan cast with foreign pleasures to beguile
Her faithful knight, and quench the heav'nly fire
That did his virtuous bosom aye inspire
With zeal unfeigned for her service true,
And send him forth in chivalrous attire,
Arm'd at all points adventures to pursue,
And wreak upon her foes his vowed vengeance due.

IX.

So as he journeyed upon the way,
Him soon the sly enchaunter [h] over-hent,
Clad like a Fairy knight in armour gay,
With painted shield, and spear right forward bent,
In knightly [i] guise and shew of [k] hardiment,
That aye prepared was for bloody fight.
Whereat the [l] Elfin knight with speeches gent
Him first saluted, who, well as he might,
Him fair salutes again, as [m] seemeth courteous knight.

[g] therefore. [h] overtook. [i] fashion. [k] courage.
[l] fairy. [m] beseemeth.

X. Then

X.

Then 'gan he ⁿ purpose frame of valiant deeds
Atchiev'd by foreign knights of ᵒ prowess great,
And mighty fame which emulation breeds
In virtuous breast, and kindleth martial heat;
Of arts and sciences for warriour ᵖ meet,
And knight that would in feats of arms excel,
Or him, who ᑫ liefer choosing calm retreat,
With Peace and gentle Virtue aye would dwell.
Who have their triumphs, like as hath Bellona fell.

XI.

These, as he said, beseemed knight to know,
And all be they in Fairy-lond y-taught,
Where every art and all fair virtues grow;
Yet various climes with various fruits are fraught,
And such in one hath full perfection ʳ raught
The which no skill may in another rear.
So gloz'd th' enchaunter 'till he hath him brought
To a huge rock, that clomb so high in air,
That from it he ˢ uneath the murmuring surge mote hear.

XII.

Thence the salt wave beyond in prospect wide
A spacious plain the false enchaunter show'd,
With goodly castles deck'd on every side,
And silver streams, that down the champain flow'd,

ⁿ discourse, or argument.   ᵒ might, valour.   ᵖ proper, fit.
ᑫ rather.   ʳ reach'd.   ˢ hardly.

And

And wash'd the vineyards that beside them stood,
And groves of myrtle; als the lamp of day
His orient beams display'd withouten cloud,
Which lightly on the glist'ning waters play,
And tinge the castles, woods, and hills with purple ray.

XIII.

So fair a landscape charm'd the wond'ring knight;
And eke the breath of morning fresh and sweet,
Inspir'd his jocund spirit with delight,
And ease of heart for soft persuasion meet.
Then him the traytor base 'gan fair entreat,
And from the rock as downward they descend,
Of that blest lond his praises 'gan repeat,
'Till he him moved hath with him to ᵗ wend;
So to the billowy shore their hasty march they bend.

XIV.

There in a painted bark all trim and gay,
Whose sails full glad embrac'd the wanton wind,
There sat a stranger ᵘ wight in quaint array,
That seem'd of various garbs ʷ attone combin'd,
Of Europe, Afric, east and western Inde.
Als round about him many creatures stood,
Of several nations, and of divers kind,
Apes, serpents, birds with human speech endow'd,
And monsters of the land, and wonders of the flood.

ᵗ to go.   ᵘ man or woman.   ʷ together.

XV. He

XV.

He was to weet a mighty traveller,
Who Curiosity thereafter ˣ hight,
And well he knew each coast and harbour fair,
And every nation's latitude and site,
And how to steer the wand'ring bark aright.
So to him strait the false enchaunter bore,
And with him likewise brought the red-cross knight:
Then fairly him besought to waft them o'er;
Swift flew the daunting bark, and reach'd the adverse shore.

XVI.

There when they landed were, them ran to greet
A bevy bright of damsels gent and gay,
Who with soft smiles, and salutation sweet,
And courteous violence would force them stay,
And rest them in their bow'r not far away;
Their bow'r, that most luxuriously was ʸ dight
With all the dainties of air, earth, and sea,
All that mote please the taste and charm the sight,
The pleasure of the board, and charm of beauty bright.

XVII.

Als might he therein hear a mingled sound
Of feast and song and laughing jollity,
That in the noise was all distinction drown'd
Of graver sense, or music's harmony.

ˣ was called.   ʸ adorned, set forth.

Yet

Yet were there some in that blithe company
That aptly could discourse of virtuous lore,
Of manners, wisdom, and sound policy;
Yet ᶻ nould they often ope their sacred store,
Ne might their voice be heard 'mid riot and uproar.

XVIII.

Thereto the joys of idleness and love,
And luxury, that besots the noblest mind,
And custom prevalent at distance drove
All sense and relish of a higher kind,
Whereby the soul to virtue is refin'd.
Instead whereof the arts of slavery
Were taught, of slavery perverse and blind,
That vainly boasts her native liberty,
Yet wears the chains of pride, of lust, and gluttony.

XIX.

Of which the red-cross knight right well aware,
Would in no wise agree with them to go,
Albeit with courtly glee their leader fair,
ᵃ Hight Politessa, him did kindly woo.
But all was false pretence, and hollow show,
False as the flow'rs which to their breasts they ty'd,
Or those which seemed in their cheeks to glow,
For both were false, and not by Nature dy'd.
False rivals of the spring, and beauty's rosy pride.

ᶻ would not.   ᵃ called.

XX. Then

XX.

Then from behind them straitway 'gan advaunce
An uncouth stripling quaintly habited,
As for some revel mask, or antic daunce,
All chequer'd o'er with yellow, blue, and red;
Als in a vizor black he shrouds his head,
The which he tossed to and fro amain,
And [b] eft his lathy falchion brandished,
As if he meant fierce battle to [c] darrain,
And like a wanton ape eft skip'd he on the plain.

XXI.

And eft about him skip'd a gaudy throng
Of youthful gallants, frolic, trim, and gay,
Chanting in careless notes their amourous song,
Match'd with like careless gests, like amourous play.
Als were they gorgeous, dress'd in rich array,
And well accepted of that female train,
Whose hearts to joy and mirth devoted aye,
Each proffer'd love receive without disdain,
And part without regret from each late-favour'd swain.

XXII.

And now they do accord in wanton daunce
To join their hands upon the flow'ry plain;
The whiles with amourous leer and eyes askaunce
Each damsel fires with love her glowing swain;

[b] often.   [c] attempt.

Vol. II.   G   'Till

'Till all-impatient of the tickling pain,
In sudden laughter forth at once they break,
And ending so their daunce, each tender twain
To shady bow'rs forthwith themselves betake,
Deep hid in myrtle groves, beside a silver lake.

XXIII.

Thereat the red-cross knight was much enmov'd,
And 'gan his heart with indignation swell,
To view in forms so made to be belov'd,
Ne faith, ne truth, ne heav'nly virtue dwell;
But lust instead, and falshood, child of hell;
And glutton sloth, and love of gay attire:
And sooth to say, them well could parallel
Their lusty ^d paramours in vain desire;
Well fitted to each dame was every gallant squire.

XXIV.

Yet when their sov'reign calls them forth to arms,
Their sov'reign, whose ^e behests they most revere,
Right wisely can they menage war's alarms,
And wield with valour great the martial spear,
So that their name is dreaded far and near.
Oh! that for Liberty they did so fight!
Then need not Fairy-land their prowess fear,
Ne give in charge to her advent'rous knight
Their friendship to beware, and sense-deluding sleight.

^d lovers.   ^f commands.

XXV.

But not for liberty they wagen war,
But solely to ᶠ aggrate their mighty lord;
For whom their dearest blood they ᵍ nillen spare,
Whenso him listeth draw the conqu'ring sword;
So is that idol vain of them ador'd,
Who ne with might beyond his meanest thrall
Endued, ne with superior wisdom stor'd,
Sees at his feet prostrated millions fall;
And with religious drad obey his princely call.

XXVI.

Thereto so high and stately was his port,
That all the petty kings him sore envy'd,
And would him imitate in any sort;
With all the mimic pageantry of pride,
And worship'd be like him, and deify'd
Of courtly sycophants and ʰ caitifs vile,
Who to those services themselves apply'd,
And in that school of servitude ere while
Had learn'd to bow and grin, and flatter, and beguile.

XXVII.

For to that seminary of fashions vain,
The rich and noble from all parts repair,
Where grown enamour'd of the gaudy train,
And courteous haviour gent and debonair,

ᶠ please.   ᵍ will not.   ʰ scoundrels.

They cast to imitate such semblaunce fair;
And deeming meanly of their native lond,
Their own rough virtues they disdain to wear,
And back returning drest by foreign hond,
Ne other matter care, ne other understond.

XXVIII.

Wherefore th' enchaunter vile, who sore was griev'd
To see the knight reject those damsels gay,
Wherewith he thought him sure to have deceiv'd,
Was minded to that court him to convey,
And daze his eyen with Majesty's bright ray:
So to a stately castle he him brought,
Which in the midst of a great garden lay,
And wisely was by cunning craftsmen wrought,
And with all riches deck'd surpassing human thought.

XXIX.

There underneath a sumptuous canopy,
That with bright ore and diamonds glitter'd far,
Sate the swoln form of royal [i] surquedry,
And deem'd itself [k] allgates some creature rare,
While its own haughty state it mote compare
With the base count'nance of the vassal fry,
That seem'd to have nor eye, nor tongue, nor ear;
Ne any sense, ne any faculty,
That did not to his throne owe servile ministry.

[i] pride.   [k] by all means; omnino.

XXX. Yet

XXX.

Yet wift he not that half that homage low
Was at a wizard's fhrine in private pay'd,
The which conducted all that goodly fhow,
And as he lift th' imperial puppet play'd,
By fecret fprings and wheels right wifely made,
That he the fubtle wires mote not [1] avize,
But deem in footh that all he did or faid,
From his own motion and free grace did rife,
And that he juftly hight immortal, great, and wife.

XXXI.

And eke to each of that fame gilded train,
That meekly round that lordly throne did ftand,
Was by that wizard ty'd a magic chain,
Whereby their actions all he mote command,
And rule with hidden influence the land.
Yet to his lord he outwardly did bend,
And thofe fame magic chains within his hand
Did feem to place, albeit by the end
He held them faft, that none them from his gripe mote rend.

XXXII.

He was to weet an old and wrinkled mage,
Deep read in all the arts of policy,
And from experience grown fo crafty fage,
That none his fecret counfels mote defcry,

---

[1] difcover, perceive.

Ne search the mines of his deep subtlety.
Thereto fair peace he lov'd and cherished;
And traffic did promote and industry,
Whereby the vulgar were in quiet fed,
And the proud lords in ease and plenty wallowed.

XXXIII.

Thence all the gorgeous splendor of the court,
^m Sith the sole bus'ness of the rich and great,
Was to that hope-built temple to resort,
And round their earthly god in glory wait,
Who with their pride to swell his royal state,
Did pour large sums of gold on every one,
Brought him by harpies fell, him to aggrate,
And torn from peasants vile, beneath the throne
Who lay deep sunk in earth, and inwardly did groan.

XXXIV.

Behold, says ARCHIMAGE, the envy'd height
Of human grandeur to the gods ally'd!
Behold yon sun of pow'r, whose glorious light,
O'er this rejoicing land out-beaming wide,
Calls up those princely flow'rs on every side;
Which like the painted daughters of the plain,
Ne toil, ne spin, ne stain their silken pride
With care, or sorrow, sith withouten pain,
Them in eternal joy those heav'nly beams maintain.

^m since.

XXXV.

Them morn and evening joy eternal greets,
And for them thousands and ten thousands ⁿ moil,
Gathering from land and ocean honied sweets
For them, who in soft indolence the while
And slumb'ring peace enjoy the luscious spoil;
And as they view around the careful bees
º Forespent with labour and incessant toil,
With the sweet contrast learn themselves to please,
And heighten by compare the luxury of ease.

XXXVI.

Ungenerous man, quoth then the Fairy knight,
That can rejoice to see another's woe!
And thou, unworthy of that glory bright,
Wherewith the gods have deck'd thy princely brow,
That doth on Sloth and Gluttony bestow
The hard-earn'd fruits of Industry and Pain,
And to the dogs the labourer's morsel throw,
Unmindful of the hand that sow'd the grain,
The poor earth-trodden root of all thy greatness vain.

XXXVII.

Oh foul abuse of sacred Majesty,
That boasteth her fair self from heav'n ysprong!
Where are the marks of thy divinity?
Truth, Mercy, Justice steady, bold and strong,

ⁿ work hard.   º quite spent.

To aid the meek, and curb oppressive wrong?
Where is the care and love of public good,
That to the people's father doth belong?
Where the vice-gerent of that bounteous God,
Who bids dispense to all, what he for all bestow'd?

XXXVIII.

Dwell'st thou not rather, like the prince of hell,
In Pandemonium, full of ugly fiends?
Dissimulation, Discord, Malice fell,
Reckless Ambition, that right onward [p] wends,
Though his wild march o'erthrow both fame and friends,
And virtue and his country; crooked Guile,
Obliquely creeping to his treach'rous ends,
And Flatt'ry, curs'd assassin, who the while
He holds the murd'rous knife, can fawn, and kiss, and smile.

XXXIX.

Then 'gan he strait unvail the mirrour bright,
The which fair [q] Una gave him heretofore,
Ere he as yet, with [r] Paynim foe to fight,
For foreign land had left his native shore.
This in his careful breast he always bore,
And on it oft would cast his wary eye;
For by it magic framed was of yore,
So that no falshood mote it well abye,
But it was plainly seen, or fearfully did fly.

---

[p] goes. [q] Una in Spenser represents Truth, see B. 1. Fairy Queen.
[r] Heathen, the usual enemy of knight-errants in Spenser.

XL. This

XL.

This on that gay affembly did he turn,
And faw confounded quite the gaudy fcene;
Saw the clofe fire that inwardly did burn,
And wafte the throbbing heart with fecret * teen;
Saw bafe dependence in the haughty mien
Of lords and princes; faw the magic chain
That each did wear, but deem'd he wore unfeen,
The whiles with count'naunce glad he hid his pain,
And homage did require from each poor lowly fwain.

XLI.

And though to that old mage they louted down,
Yet did they dearly wifh for his decay:
Als trembled he, and aye upon the throne
Of his great lord his tott'ring fteps did ftay,
And oft behind him fkulk'd for great difmay;
Als fhook the throne, when fo the villain crew,
That underneath opprefs'd and groveling lay,
Impatient of the grievous burthen grew,
And loudly for redrefs and liberty did fue.

XLII.

There mote he likewife fee a ribbald train
Of dancers, broid'rers, flaves of luxury,
Who caft o'er all thofe lords and ladies vain
A veil of femblaunce fair, and richeft dye,

---

* pain, anguifh.

That none their inward bafenefs mote defcry.
But nought was hidden from that mirrour bright,
Which when falfe ARCHIMAGO 'gan efpy,
He feared for himfelf, and warn'd the knight
From fo detefted place to maken fpeedy flight.

XLIII.

So on he paffed, till he comen hath
To a fmall river, that full flow did glide,
As it uneath mote find its watry path
For ftones and rubbifh, that did choak its tide,
So lay the mould'ring piles on every fide,
Seem'd there a goodly city once had been,
Albeit now fallen were her royal pride,
Yet more her auncient greatnefs ftill be feen,
Still from her ruins prov'd the world's imperial queen.

XLIV.

For the rich fpoil of all the continents,
The boaft of art and nature there was brought,
Corinthian brafs, Ægyptian monuments,
With hieroglyphic fculptures all inwrought,
And Parian marbles, by Greek artifts taught
To counterfeit the forms of heroes old,
And fet before the eye of fober thought
Lycurgus, Homer, and Alcides bold.
All thefe and many more that may not here be told.

XLV. There

XLV.

There in the middest of a ruin'd pile,
That seem'd a theatre of circuit vast,
Where thousands might be seated, he erewhile
Discover'd hath an uncouth trophy plac'd;
Seem'd a huge heap of stone together cast
In nice disorder and wild symmetry,
Urns, broken freezes, statues half defac'd,
And pedestals with antique imagery
Emboss'd, and pillars huge of costly porphyry.

XLVI.

Aloft on this strange basis was † ypight
With girlonds gay adorn'd a golden chair,
In which aye smiling with self-bred delight,
In careless pride reclin'd a lady fair,
And to soft music lent her idle ear;
The which with pleasure so did her enthrall,
That for aught else she had but little care,
For wealth, or fame, or honour feminal,
Or gentle love, sole king of pleasures natural.

XLVII.

Als by her side, in richest robes array'd,
An eunuch sate, of visage pale and dead,
Unseemly paramour for royal maid!
Yet him she courted oft and honoured,

† placed.

And oft would by her place in princely ^u sted,
Though from the dregs of earth he springen were,
And oft with regal crowns she deck'd his head,
And oft, to sooth her vain and foolish ear,
She bade him the great names of mighty ^w Kesars bear.

XLVIII.

Thereto herself a pompous title bore,
For she was vain of her great aunceſtry,
But vainer still of that prodigious store
Of arts and learning, which she vaunts to lie
In the rich archives of her treasury.
These she to strangers oftentimes would shew,
With grave demean and solemn vanity,
Then proudly claim as to her merit due,
The venerable praise and title of Vertù.

XLIX.

Vertù she was ^x yclep'd, and held her court
With outward shews of pomp and majesty,
To which natheless few others did resort,
But men of base and vulgar industry,
Or such perdy as of them cozen'd be,
Mimes, fiddlers, pipers, eunuchs squeaking fine,
Painters and builders, sons of masonry,
Who well could measure with the rule and line,
And all the orders five right craftily define.

^u seat or place. ^w emperors. ^x called or named.

L.

But other skill of cunning architect,
How to contrive the house for dwelling best,
With self-sufficient scorn they wont neglect,
As corresponding with their purpose least;
And herein be they copied of the rest,
Who aye pretending love of science fair,
And gen'rous purpose to adorn the breast
With lib'ral arts, to Vertù's court repair,
Yet nought but tunes and names, and coins away do bear.

LI.

For long, to visit her once-honour'd seat
The studious sons of learning have forbore:
Who whilom thither ran with pilgrim feet
Her venerable reliques to adore,
And load their bosoms with the sacred store,
Whereof the world large treasure yet enjoys.
But [y] sithence she declin'd from wisdom's lore,
They left her to display her pompous toys
To virtuosi vain, and wonder-gaping boys.

LII.

Forthy to her a num'rous train doth [z] long
Of ushers in her court well practised,
Who aye about the monied stranger throng,
Off'ring with shews of courteous [a] bountihed

---

[y] since.   [z] belong.   [a] good-nature or civility.

Him

Him through the rich apartments all to lead,
And shew him all the wonders of her state,
Whose names and price they wisely can ^b areed,
And tell of coins of old and modern date,
And pictures false and true right well discriminate.

LIII.

Als are they named after him, whose tongue
Shook the dictator in his curule chair,
And thund'ring through the Roman senate, rung
His bold Philippics in Antonius' ear ;
Which when the Fairy heard, he sigh'd full dear,
And casting round his quick discerning eye,
At every ^c deal he dropt a manly tear,
As he the stately buildings mote descry,
Baths, theatres, and fanes in mould'ring fragments lie.

LIV.

And, oh! imperial city! then he said,
How art thou tumbled from thine Alpine throne!
Whereon, like Jove on high Olympus' head,
Thou sittedst erst unequall'd and alone,
And madest through the world thy greatness known ;
While from the western isles, to Indus' shore,
From seven-mouth'd Nilus, to the frozen Don,
Thy dradded bolts the strong-pounc'd Eagle bore
And taught the nations round thy Fasces to adore.

^b relate or declare. Those under sort of antiquarians, who go about with strangers to shew them the antiquities, &c. of Rome, are called Ciceroni. ^c At every turn, every now and then.

LV. And

LV.

And doth among thy reliques nought remain,
No little portion of that haughty spright,
Which made thee whilom scorn soft Pleasure's chain,
And in free Virtue place thy chief delight,
Whereby through ages shone thy glory bright?
And is there nought remaining to confound
Those, who regardless of thy woeful plight,
With idle wonder view thy ruins round,
And without thought survey thy memorable wound?

LVI.

Arise, thou genuine Cicero, and declare
That all these mighty ruins scatter'd wide,
The sepulchres of Roman virtue were,
And trophies vast of Luxury and Pride,
Those fell diseases whereof Rome erst dy'd.
And do you then with vile mechanic thought
Your course, ye sons of Fairy, hither guide,
That ye those gay refinements may be taught,
Which Liberty's fair lond to shame and thraldom brought?

LVII.

Let Rome those vassal arts now meanly boast,
Which to her vanquish'd thralls she erst resign'd;
Ye who enjoy that freedom she has lost,
That great prerogative of human-kind,

Close

Close to your heart the precious jewel bind,
And learn the rich possession to maintain,
Learn Virtue, Justice, Constancy of Mind,
Not to be mov'd by Fear or Pleasure's train;
Be these your arts, ye brave, these only are humane.

LVIII.

As he thus spake, th' enchaunter half asham'd
Wist not what fitting answer to devise,
Als was his caitive heart well-nigh inflam'd,
By that same knight so virtuous, brave, and wise.
That long he doubts him farther to entice.
But he was harden'd and remorseless grown,
Through practice old of villainy and vice;
So to his former wiles he turns him soon,
As in another place hereafter shall be shown.

THE INSTITUTION OF THE ORDER OF THE GARTER.

A DRAMATIC POEM.

By the SAME.

―― *Lectos ex omnibus oris*
Evebis; & meritum, non quæ cunabula quæris,
Et qualis; non unde satus: sub teste benigno
Vivitur; egregios invitant præmia mores. CLAUD.

HONI SOIT QUI MAL Y PENSE.

Dramatis Personæ.

Edward the Third, King of England, &c.
Philippa, Queen of England, &c.
Edward, Prince of Wales.
John, * King of France, &c.

Spirits. { Genius of England.
{ Bards.
{ Druids.

Heralds, Attendants, &c.

SCENE,

Windsor Park, with a Prospect of the Castle.

---

* The order of the Garter was instituted on St. George's day, the 23d of April, 1350. King John came into England in 1357. I have taken the advantage of the licence usually allowed to poets, of departing a little from chronology; and have postponed for a few years the institution of this order, for the sake of rendering that solemnity more august, by introducing King John of France, who, though a prisoner, was treated both by Edward and his son the prince of Wales, with all the regard due to the quality and virtue of so great a prince. To alleviate his captivity, Edward entertained him and the other French prisoners with diversions of various kinds; among which, a tournament he held at Windsor on the 23d of April, to solemnize the feast of St. George, the patron of the order of the Garter, held the chief place; and was, as Rapin tells us, the most sumptuous and magnificent that had ever been seen in England. The duke of Brabant, with several other sovereign princes, and an infinite number of knights of all nations were present, and splendidly entertained.

THE

THE INSTITUTION OF THE ORDER of the GARTER.

SCENE, WINDSOR PARK.

Flourish of aërial music *at a distance, after which the following verses are sung in the air by* SPIRITS, *while the* GENIUS *of* England *descends.*

First SPIRIT.

HITHER, all ye heav'nly pow'rs,
From your empyreal bow'rs;
From the fields for ever gay,
From the star-pav'd milky way,
From the moon's relucent horn,
From the star that wakes the morn;
From the bow, whose mingling dyes
Sweetly chear the frowning skies;
From the silver cloud that sails
Shadowy o'er the darken'd vales;
From th' Elysiums of the sky,
Spirits immortal, hither fly!

CHORUS

Chorus of Spirits.

Fly, and through the limpid air
Guard in pomp the sliding car,
Which to his terrestrial throne
Wafts Britannia's Genius down.

Second Spirit.

Hither, all ye heav'nly pow'rs!
From your empyreal bow'rs!
Chiefly ye, whose brows divine
Crown'd with starry circlets shine;
Who in various labours try'd,
Once Britannia's strength and pride,
Now in everlasting rest
Share the glories of the blest!
Peers and nobles of the sky,
Spirits immortal, hither fly!

Chorus of Spirits.

Fly, and thro' the limpid air
Guard in pomp the sliding car,
Which to his terrestrial throne
Wafts Britannia's Genius down.

Third Spirit.

Hither too, ye tuneful throng,
Masters of enchanting song,
Sacred bards! whose rapt'rous strains
Sooth the toiling hero's pains,
Sooth the patriot's gen'rous cares;
Sweetly through their ravish'd ears

Whisp'ring

Whisp'ring to th' immortal mind
Heav'nly visions, hopes refin'd;
Hopes of endless peace and fame,
Safe from envy's blasting flame;
Pure, sincere, in those abodes,
Where to throngs of list'ning gods,
Hymning bards, to virtue's praise,
Tune their never-dying lays.
Sweet encomiasts of the sky,
Spirits immortal, hither fly!

CHORUS OF SPIRITS.

Fly, and charm the limpid air,
While the softly-sliding car,
To his sea-encircled throne
Wafts Britannia's Genius down.

Chorus of BARDS *descend, dress'd in long flowing sky-colour'd robes spangled with stars, with garlands of oaken boughs upon their heads, and golden harps in their hands, made like the* Welch, *or old British harp. Before they appear, they sing the chorus, and afterwards, as they descend, the following songs; at the last stanza of which, the chariot of the* GENIUS *appears, and descends gradually all the while that and the grand chorus is singing.*

CHORUS OF BARDS.

Gentle Spirit, we obey;
Thus along th' ætherial way,
We attend our monarch's car;
Thus we charm the silent air.

SONG.

First Bard.

Ye southern gales, that ever fly
  In frolic April's vernal train,
Who, as ye skim along the sky,
  Dip your light pinions in the main;
Then shake them fraught with genial show'rs
O'er blooming Flora's primrose-bow'rs;

2.

Now cease awhile your wanton sport,
  Now drive each threat'ning cloud away;
Then to the flow'ry vale resort,
  And hither all its sweets convey;
And ever as ye dance along,
With softest murmurs aid our song.

SONG II.

Second Bard.

But lo! fair Windsor's tow'rs appear,
  And hills with spreading oaks imbrown'd!
Hark! hark! the voice of joy I hear,
  Sung by a thousand echoes round;
And now I view a glitt'ring train,
In triumph march o'er yonder plain.

Grand CHORUS OF SPIRITS and BARDS.
Hail mighty nation! ever fam'd in war!
Lo! heav'n descends thy festivals to share;
To view those heroes, whose immortal praise
Celestial bards shall sing in living lays.

At the conclusion of this chorus, the GENIUS *alights from his chariot, the front of which, resembling the head of a man of war, is adorned with a carved lion; holding before his breast the arms of England, as they were borne by* Edward. *Behind, on a rais'd seat, sits the* GENIUS, *leaning upon an anchor of silver, and bearing in his right hand the* vindicta, *or wand of enfranchisement, and in his left a roll of parchment, upon which is written, in large letters of gold,* MAGNA CHARTA. *On his head is a* corona rostrata, *or naval crown; and his robe, of a sea-green colour, is embroidered with cornucopias and golden tridents.*

GENIUS.

Disdain not, ye blest denizens of air,
To breathe this grosser atmosphere awhile,
Your service I shall need; mean time resort
To yon imperial palace, and in air
Draw up your squadrons in a radiant orb,
Suspended o'er those lofty battlements,
Like the bright halo that invests the moon,
Or Saturn's lucid ring: thence shed benign
Your choicest influence on the noble train,
There on this solemn day assembled round
The throne of British Edward: I awhile
Must here await th' approach of other spirits,

Sage Druids, Britain's old philosophers;
Fetch'd by my summons from the western isles,
That, scatter'd o'er the rough Hibernian flood,
Seem like huge fragments by the wild wave torn
From stormy Scotland, and the Cambrian shore.
There, from the world retir'd, in sacred shades,
Chiefly where Breint and Meinai wash'd the oaks
Of ancient Mona, their academies
And schools of sage and moral discipline
They held; and to the neighb'ring Britons round,
From their rever'd tribunals, holy mounts,
Dispens'd at once their oracles and laws.
'Till fierce Paulinus, and his Roman bands,
Them and their gods defying, drove them thence
To seek for shelter in Hibernian shades.
Yet still enamour'd of their ancient haunts,
Unseen of mortal eyes, they hover round
Their ruin'd altars, consecrated hills,
Once girt with spreading oaks, mysterious rows
Of rude enormous obelisks, that rise
Orb within orb, stupendous monuments
Of artless architecture, such as now
Oft times amaze the wand'ring traveller,
By the pale moon discern'd on Sarum's plain.
But hence, aërial spirits: lo, they come!

Here the SPIRITS *and* BARDS, *together with the chariot of the* GENIUS, *reascend, and at the same time the* DRUIDS *enter, cloath'd in dark-colour'd coarse stuff gowns;*
which

which before hang no lower than the knee, but behind almost touch the ground. The sleeves of these gowns reach down below the elbow, and from behind comes up a sort of hood or cowle, which hangs loose about the head and forehead From the left shoulder hangs in a string a kind of pouch, or scrip, and rests on the right hip. In their right hands they hold a staff, and in their left an oaken branch. Their beards are very large and long, reaching below their waists. Their legs are naked, and their feet shod with sandals, which are fastened by thongs wound about the foot and the small of the leg [a].

Enter DRUIDS.

Chief DRUID.

Inform us, happy spirit, protecting pow'r
Of this our ancient country, wherefore now
From our sequester'd vallies, pensive groves,
And dark recesses, thou hast summon'd us
To wait thy orders on this flow'ry hill?

GENIUS.

A great event, sage Druids, that no less
Imports than this your ancient country's fame,
From contemplation, and your silent shades,
Calls you to meet me on this flow'ry hill.

Know, in yon castle, whose proud battlements
Sit like a regal crown upon the brow
Of this high-climbing lawn, doth Edward hold
This day his solemn session, to receive

[a] See a cut of the chief Druid, in Rowland's Mona Antiqua Restaurata, taken from a statue, p. 65.

The

The pleas of all th' aspiring candidates,
Who, summon'd by the ^b heralds public voice,
To Windsor, as to Fame's bright temple, haste
From every shore; the noble, wise, and brave,
Knights, senators, and statesmen, lords and kings;
Ambitious each to gain the splendid prize,
By Edward promis'd to transcendent worth.
For who of mortals is too great and high
In the career of virtue to contend?
Of these, selecting the most glorious names,
Doth England's monarch purpose to compose
A princely brotherhood, himself the chief,
And worthy sov'reign of th' illustrious band;
A band of heroes, lifted in the cause
Of honour, virtue, and celestial truth,
Under the name and holy patronage
Of Cappadocian GEORGE, Britannia's saint.

 Such is the plan by gen'rous Edward form'd;
A plan of glory, that, beyond the reach
Of his own conqu'ring arms, shall propagate

 [b] Edward having communicated his intention of instituting the order of the GARTER to the great council of his realm, and having received their approbation, dispatched his heralds to several parts of Europe, to invite all that were eminent for military virtue, &c. to be present at its institution. And his queen Philippa, on her part, assembled a train of 300 of the fairest ladies to grace the solemnity, and add to its magnificence.

The fov'reignty of Britain, and erect
Her monarchs into judges of mankind.
   But from this day's decisions, from the choice
Of his first collegues, shall succeeding times
Of Edward judge, and on his fame pronounce.
For dignities and titles, when misplac'd
Upon the vicious, the corrupt and vile,
Like princely virgins to low peasants match'd,
Descend from their nobility, and, foil'd
By base alliance, not their pride alone
And native splendor lose, but shame retort
Ev'n on the sacred throne, from whence they sprung.
So may the lustre of this order bright,
This eldest child of chivalry be stain'd,
If at her first espousals, her great sire,
Caught by the specious outsides, that deceive
And captivate the world, admit the suit
Of vain pretenders void of real worth;
Light empty bubbles, by the wanton gale
Of fortune swell'd, and only form'd to dance
And glitter in the sun-shine of a court.
   Begin we then with Edward; first let him
At his own high tribunal undergo
The rigid inquisition —— I for this
Have left my lucid star-encircled throne:
For this, immortal sages, have requir'd
Your wise and prudent ministry, well skill'd
In various science, and the human heart.

Search Edward's to the bottom: found the depths
And shallows of his soul; if he possess
That first of regal talents, to discern
With quick-ey'd penetration, through the veil
Of art, each character's intrinsic worth,
And all the labyrinths of the human mind.
Nor blush for this good end yourselves to wear
Fallacious forms, to plead the cause of false
But specious merit: at his throne appear
In borrow'd shapes, and there with artful guile,
When the shrill trumpet cites the candidates,
Urge your pretensions: all the pow'r employ
Of wit and eloquence: Edward, I trust,
The trial shall abide; which shall but tend
To manifest, that not from arrogance,
But conscious virtue, hath he thus assum'd
Above all other kings, to be the judge
And great rewarder of heroic deeds.
Nor wholly unassisted will I leave
My royal charge, but with blest influence clear
His intellectual eye from the dim mists
It haply hath contracted from a long
Unebbing current of felicity,
Unhop'd, unequall'd triumphs, from the view
Of captive monarchs, and the glitt'ring throng,
Who at his summons from all climates come,
To take, as from their sov'reign, honours new,

When heav'n tries mortals in unusual ways,
'Tis fit it should afford unusual aid.
   Now, sages, to yon spreading oaks retire,
There wait my summons; and mean time advise
How best to execute the task enjoin'd.
[Ex. Gen. and Druids.

The SCENE *changes to a large room in the castle (*St. George's Hall*) at the upper end of which is a royal canopy with the figure of St.* GEORGE, *and the motto of the Garter,* HONI SOIT QUI MAL Y PENSE, *beneath it embroider'd in gold. Under this canopy appears, seated on an elevation of two or three steps, king* Edward, *in the habit of the order of the Garter, with a scepter in his right hand, and a globe in his left. On his left hand is seated queen* Philippa, *with a crown upon her head, and dress'd in a royal mantle of crimson velvet, powder'd with embroider'd garters, and an enamel'd* c *garter bound like a bracelet upon her left arm. By her stand a great number of ladies very richly dress'd. On* Edward's *right hand is seated king* John, *in the imperial robes of* France; *and on the same side, but a step lower, sits* Edward *the Black Prince, in the robes belonging to the Prince of* Wales. *Next to queen* Philippa *are seated the rest of* Edward's *children; and next to the Black Prince, on the other side, stand the French prisoners, and a great number of lords, &c. richly dress'd.*

On the floor, at some distance, stands Garter king at arms in the habit of his office, holding in his hand a Garter, with the grand collar of the order. Near him stand other heralds, ushers, attendants, &c.

  c That the ladies of the knights of the Garter wore this ensign of the order upon their left arms, may be seen in Ashmole's History of the Garter.

Flourish

Flourish of trumpets, kettle-drums, &c. After which Edward, rising up from his throne, addresses himself to the assembly.

EDWARD.

That hither from your distant residence,
By solemn invitation, noble guests,
I have entreated your illustrious train,
Misconstrue not to levity and pride,
Or ostentatious vain magnificence,
Unworthy the grave majesty of kings,
Unworthy your attention, my renown.
This bright assemblage of the wise, the brave,
The noble, the magnificent, the fair,
The ornaments of Europe, have I sought
To grace the pomp of Virtue, to adorn
With noblest off'rings her unspotted shrine,
Attracting thus to her divine commands
The aweful veneration of mankind.
This was the cause, great princes, this the call,
The voice of Virtue, not of England's king,
That with respectful zeal ye hear'd and follow'd:
From Burgundy's rich vineyards; from the meads
Of Hainault and Brabant; the rocky wave
Of Danube; from Germania's warlike tow'rs,
Imperial mother of an hundred states;
From Spain, long exercis'd by Moorish arms;
From Italy's fair princedoms, and the walls
Of sea-wash'd Venice, Adria's haughty spouse.

With

With me then, all ye virtuous, by what stile
Recorded in the registers of fame,
Knights, senators, or soldiers, ermin'd lords,
Or scepter'd princes; from whatever clime
Ye come, ennobled by heroic acts,
With me unite the splendor of your names
To dignify th' erection of a new
And noble order, which to heav'n's high praise,
And to heav'n's champion, Cappadocian GEORGE,
On this his holy festival I mean
To found a recompence for worthiest deeds.
Thus as the orient sun, ador'd of old
By prostrate Persia, ow'd his deity
Less to that genial and benignant heat
That cherishes and warms the seeds of life,
Than to those gorgeous beams, that deck with gold
And crimson the gay portals of the morn;
So shall this rising order owe its fame
And brightest lustre to the splendid train
Of lords and purpled princes, who are met
This day to usher and adorn its birth.

Nor deem that to allure heroic minds,
My private int'rests partially to serve,
To lift the valiant in ambition's cause,
And form a league of conquest, I have laid
In subtle policy this great design;

ASHAM'D

> [d] ASHAM'D BE HE WHO WITH MALIGNANT EYE
> SO READS MY PURPOSE: and be he accurs'd
> Whoe'er in after-times shall so pervert
> This sacred institution. To the world
> I here consign it, to the good and great
> Of every age and clime, and them alone.

Now

[d] Edward being engaged in a war with France, for the obtaining that crown, in order to draw into England great multitudes of foreigners, with whom he might negotiate either for their personal service, or aids of troops to assist him in that undertaking, ordered, during the truce that then subsisted between the two crowns, publication to be made of a great tournament, to be held at Windsor; an expedient, says Rapin, which could not fail of success, because it was entirely agreeable to the taste of that age. Accordingly many persons of distinction came over, to all of whom he gave an honourable reception, caressing them in such a manner that they could never sufficiently admire his politeness, magnificence, and liberality. To render these entertainments the more solemn, and to free himself also from the ceremonies, to which the difference of rank and condition would have subjected him, he caused a circular hall of boards to be run up at Windsor, 200 feet in diameter. There it was that he feasted all the knights at one table, which was called the Round Table, in memory of the great Arthur, who, as it is pretended, instituted an order of knighthood by that name. Next year he caused a more solid building to be erected, that he might continue yearly the same diversions. During that time he treated with these several lords about the aids, wherewith each could furnish him, in proportion to his forces. His rival, king Philip, could not see without jealousy, Spaniards, Italians, Germans, Flemings, and Frenchmen themselves flock to England to assist at these tournaments. He suspected some hidden design in these entertainments, and to break Edward's mea-

sures,

Now sound the trumpet; bid the candidates
With confidence appear, and urge their claims.

Flourish of trumpets, &c. which is answered by another trumpet from without; then enter a grandee of Spain, *magnificently attir'd in the* Spanish *habit, holding in his hand the pedigree of his family, and preceded by heralds, &c. bearing atchievements, banners, coats of armour, helmets, gauntlets, spurs, &c.*

SPANIARD.

Illustrious monarch! emp'ror of the isles!
My name is Guzman—from those heroes sprung,

sures, caused the like to be published in his dominions; which meeting with success, proved a countermine to Edward's main design, so that he did not long continue to keep up his round table. From thence, however, it is generally agreed, he took the first hint of instituting the order of the Garter. But as his purpose in erecting this order was very different from that which had induced him to revive Arthur's round table, as he had in this no private views, no ambitious scheme of engaging such as should be admitted into this fraternity to assist him in his wars, he thought proper, in order to obviate the like jealousies and suspicion as had alarmed king Philip, to signify by his motto the purity of his intentions, and to retort shame upon all those who should put any malignant construction upon his design in instituting this order. This therefore I take to be the true meaning and import of the famous motto HONI SOIT QUI MAL Y PENSE. The not understanding the purport of which, gave rise, in all probability, to that vulgar story of the countess of Salisbury's garter, rejected by all the best writers.

Who with Pelagio 'mid th' Asturian rocks
Against th' invasion of unnumber'd Moors,
Maintain'd the fame and empire of the Goths,
And founded at Oviedo once again
The Spanish monarchy and Cath'lic faith,
Transporting from the mountain's dreary womb
To glitt'ring temples her most holy altars.
Thence on the bordering Moor their valiant sons
Waging incessant war, ere long regain'd
Their ancient realms of Leon, Arragon,
And rich Castilia: in which great exploits
My brave progenitors, by valour, zeal,
And loyalty distinguish'd, from their kings
Gain'd those high honours, princely signories,
And proud prerogatives, which have extoll'd
The name of Guzman to such envy'd grandeur,
That scarce above it towers the regal throne.

   These honours undiminish'd, undefil'd,
To me deliver'd down, might well content
A vulgar mind; but spirits highly born
Are full of gen'rous and aspiring thoughts;
And use the vantage ground of rank and pow'r
But to ascend still higher. Thus I come
Thy GARTER to sollicit; pleas'd, great prince,
With thee to be enroll'd thy brother knight,
And fearing no repulse. Nobility,
As nearest in her orbit, first receives
The beams of majesty; alone can bear

The

The fullness of that glory, which o'erpow'rs
Inferior natures.   Virtue's self would blush,
Did she at once approach too near the throne;
But the young eagle borne amid the blaze
Of glancing lightnings, with undazzled eye
Soars to the courts of heav'n, and perches bold
On the bright sceptre of imperial Jove.
   The greatest king is he, who is the king
Of greatest subjects.   Seek'st thou to advance
The glory of thy order? To thyself
Associate those, whose high-exalted names
For ages past from Envy's self have forc'd
Habitual veneration, never paid
To new and upstart merit.   Such am I,
Whose pure and gen'rous blood descending down
From nobler fountains, in its course enrich'd
By glorious mixtures with each royal stream
That fair Iberia boasts, might ev'n pretend
To thy alliance, Edward.   View this scroll,
The faithful blazon of my ancient line,
A line of potentates, whose every son
Deserv'd to wear the GARTER I demand.
In me their representative, the heir
Of all their honours, son of their renown,
Do thou reward their virtues: in their names
I claim, and on hereditary right,
The right of monarchs, Edward, rest my plea.

EDWARD.

EDWARD.

The high desert of thy renown'd forefathers
Well hast thou shewn; but hast thou therefore prov'd
Thyself deserving to be call'd their son?
To thee their prosp'rous virtues have indeed
Transmitted lineal rank, and titles proud,
By them more hardly gain'd; for which thou stand'st
To custom and th' indulgence of thy country
Indebted, Guzman, in a large account;
Which thou must first discharge by noble deeds,
Ere thou canst stile those dignities thine own.
This if thou hast not paid, why dost thou seek,
Like thriftless prodigals, to swell the debt,
And overwhelm thyself with obligations?

 Virtue is honour, and the noblest titles
Are but the public stamps set on the ore
To ascertain its value to mankind.
It were a kind of treason to my crown,
To mark base metal with the royal impress,
And put off lazy pride in virtue's name.

 Would'st thou attain my GARTER? Seek it there
Where thy heroic ancestors acquir'd
Their glorious honours, in th' embattled field
Among the squadrons of the warlike Moors:
Or in the council of thy king, by truth
And wisdom equal to th' important trust.
Be what thy fathers were, and then return

To ask the pledge of merit from my hand,
And be the fit companion of a king. [*Exit* Spaniard.

Flourish of trumpets, &c. which, as before, is answer'd by another trumpet from without; then enter an usurer and senator of Genoa *(at that time the bank of* Europe*) dress'd in his senatorial gown of black velvet, profusely, but awkwardly adorn'd with jewels, pearls, and diamond necklaces, pendents, bracelets, rings, such as he may be supposed to have received as pawns, and to wear rather as marks of his great riches, than as ornaments of his dress. He is attended by a large train of people of every profession, appearing to be his debtors, by their abject and timid countenances; at the head of whom, and next to the usurer, marches a scrivener, bearing a large bundle of bonds, mortgages, &c.*

GENOESE.

From Genoa the opulent, the bank
And treasury of the world, most puissant king,
Invited by thy heralds, am I come
To claim the honour by thy promise due,
Due by thy justice to superior worth;
Due then to me, great Edward, who possess
That object of the toils, the cares, the vows
Of all mankind, that comprehensive good,
Source of all pow'r and grandeur, boundless wealth.

Behold yon glitt'ring train, whose sumptuous pride,
Bright with the treasure of each precious mine,
Invests with glory thy imperial throne:
Whence is their dignity? The ray august,
That awes and dazzles the respectful crowd,

Proceeds it from nobility, from virtue,
Their wisdom, or their valour, or their fame?
Comes it not rather from the beaming ore?
The diamond's star-like radiance? Wealth, O king,
Wealth is the sun that decks the gorgeous scene;
That cherishes, adorns, and calls to view,
These princely flowers of honour, virtue, fame,
Which in the shades of poverty were lost.
Whatever men desire or venerate,
On wealth attends; ev'n empire's self is bought.
Nor could the mighty Julius have attain'd
By wisdom or by valour sov'reign power,
Had not the gold of vanquish'd Gaul subdu'd
The liberties of Rome. On wretched want,
Contempt and narrow-soul'd dependence wait.
Ev'n kings, of necessary wealth depriv'd,
In powerless indigence lose all respect,
All homage from their subjects: while the rich,
Like gods ador'd, o'er every neck extend
Their potent sceptres, and in golden chains
Fierce Faction and rebellious Freedom bind.

 The glory, strength, importance of a realm,
Is measur'd by its riches: Venice thus,
Thus Genoa's petty state out-balances,
In Europe's scale, the boundless wilds that cloath
With tributary furs the Russian Czar.
With like pre-eminence exalted shines

In every land above the proudeſt names,
The bleſt poſſeſſor of all-worſhip'd gold.

   My birth or rank I boaſt not here, though born
A ſenator of Genoa. The deſert,
On which I found my claim, is all my own;
To have adorn'd and dignify'd the ſtate
Of my declining houſe with greater wealth
Than e'er my thriftleſs anceſtors poſſeſs'd;
Whoſe richeſt acquiſitions were but ſprigs
Of barren laurel, or the flaunting rags
Of ſome torn enſign, to their needy ſon
A worthleſs heritage. Yet not to ſwell
My narrow fortunes would my ſoul deſcend
To the baſe methods of ignoble trade,
And vulgar mercantile purſuit of gain.
Mine were the noble arts of raiſing gold
From gold, of nurſing and improving wealth
By gainful uſe; arts practis'd heretofore
By ſenators and ſages of old Rome,
Illuſtrious Craſſus, and wiſe Seneca.
Thus have I grac'd the ſplendor of my name
With ſuitable poſſeſſions; thus I hold
In firm ſubjection to my will the poor
Of every rank and order, ſoldier, prieſt,
The vent'rous merchant, and the ſumptuous lord,
Who in a lower vaſſalage to me,
Than to thy ſceptre, Edward, bow their heads,
Pledging their lands and liberties for gold.

Hence am I bold to stand before thy throne
A candidate for glory's highest prize:
And let me add, that policy alone
Should teach thy prudence to approve my claim;
Should teach thee in thy subjects to excite,
By honours on superior wealth bestow'd,
An useful emulation to be rich:
Which once inspir'd, thy Albion shall become
The first of nations, thou the first of kings.

     EDWARD.

 Hadst thou by op'ning to thy native land
The golden veins of commerce, by employing
The useful hands of industry in works
Of national advantage, by uniting
Remotest regions in the friendly bands
And honest intercourse of mutual trade;
Hadst thou by these humane and generous arts,
Which thy mistaken pride so much disdains,
Enrich'd at once thy country and thy self,
Then not unworthy hadst thou been to wear
The brightest marks of honour; but thy wealth,
The base-born child of sordid usury,
That foe to commerce, nurse of idleness,
Stains and degrades thee from thy noble birth;
Nor in the usurer can I discern
The senator of Genoa.——To enlarge
The mind with gen'rous sentiments, to raise
Its aims by virtuous emulation, here

             I sit;

I fit; but not to gild with honour's beams
That selfish passion which congeals the heart,
And stops the streams of sweet benevolence,
Mean avarice, the vice of narrowest souls,
Incapable of glory.—Wealth, thou say'st,
Can buy ev'n empire, and to Julius gave
Dominion o'er his country——Fatal gift,
And ruinous to both! But what to Rome,
What to that Cæsar's successors avail'd
The boundless treasures of the ravag'd world,
When they had lost their virtue? Did not soon
The valiant sons of poverty, the Goths,
The Huns and Vandals, from their barren hills
And rugged woods descending, to their steel
Subject the Roman gold? Yet I deny not
The pow'r and use of riches: to the wise
And good, in public or in private life,
They are the means of virtue, and best serve
The noblest purposes; but in the use,
Not in the bare possession, lies the merit.
Shew me thy merit then, thy bounteous acts,
Public munificence, or private alms,
The hungry, and the naked, and the sick,
Sustain'd and cherish'd by thy saving hand;
Plead this, and I allow thy worthy claim,
For this is virtue, and deserves reward..

[*Ex.* Gen.

Flourish

Flourish of trumpets, &c. which is answered by a symphony of flutes, violins, &c. playing a light amorous air; then appears a Neapolitan *courtier, a favourite of queen* Joan, *who then reigned at* Naples, *and whose court was the most debauch'd and dissolute of that age. He comes in with a gay and affected gesture, and is dress'd in loose silken robes, rich, but finical and effeminate; on his hair, which is curl'd and spread all over his shoulders down to the middle of his back, he wears a chaplet of roses, and is attended by a train of beautiful boys, habited like cupids, and musicians, who, as he marches towards the throne, continue playing their soft and wanton airs.*

NEAPOLITAN.

Not on my wealth, nor on my noble blood,
Shall I presume to claim thy royal gift,
Auspicious prince, but on the skill to give
That splendor to nobility and wealth,
That elegance of taste, from which alone
Their value they derive; of this to judge,
This to direct, I boast, fit arbiter
Of all refin'd delights.—But chief to kings
My happy talents I devote; on them
My genius waits with duteous care, and wafts
The golden cup of pleasure to their lips,
Like Ganymede before the throne of Jove.
And who indeed would wish to be a god
Only to thunder, and to hear the pray'rs
Of clam'rous suitors? 'Tis the nectar'd feast,
The dance of Graces, and the wanton charms
Of Venus, sporting with the Smiles and Loves,

That make the court of heav'n a blest abode.
Far happier were the meanest peasant's lot,
Who sleeps or sings in careless ease beneath
The sun-burnt hay-cock, or the flow'ry thorn,
Than to be plac'd on high in anxious pride,
The purple drudge, and slave of tiresome state,
If to superior pow'r superior means
Of joy were not annex'd, and larger scope
For every wish the lavish heart can form:
If the soft hand of pleasure did not wreathe
Around the royal diadem, whose weight
Oppressive loads the monarch's aching brow,
Her fairest growth of ever-blooming flow'rs.

  On thee, victorious prince, propitious Fortune
Hath pour'd her richest gifts, renown and wealth,
And greatness equal to thy mighty mind;
One only bliss is wanting to thy court,
Voluptuous elegance; the lovely child
Of ease and opulence; that never comes,
But like a bird of summer to attend
The brightest sun-shine of a glorious state.
To her, and her alone, belongs the task,
By learned delicacy to remove
What yet remains in this thy ancient realm
Of Gothic barbarism, the rust of war,
And valiant ignorance.—Her artful hand
Thy rugged Britons shall refine, and teach
More courtly manners, to their sov'reign's will

Politely

Politely pliant: do but thou command
Thy willing servant, with thy favours grac'd,
From fair Joanna's ever-smiling court,
Under whose happy influence I was train'd,
From polish'd Naples, her delightful seat,
The blooming goddess to transport, with all
Her train of joys, and fix them here beneath
Thy great protection.—But perhaps thou fear'st
The voice of censure, and the grave reproof
Of moralizing dullness: idle fear!
The vulgar herd, indeed, religious craft
And policy of state have well confin'd
With wise severity to rigid laws:
Else would that headstrong beast the multitude
Forget obedience, and its rider's voice
Disdain. But shall the rider put a curb
In his own mouth? The laws that kings have made
Shall they restrain the makers? Edward, no!
For thee indulgent justice shall relax
Her harsh decrees, and piety shall wait
To give her rev'rend sanction to thy will.
'Tis thine to rove at large through nature's field,
Crop ev'ry flow'r, and taste of every fruit;
By sweet variety provoking still
The languid appetite to new desires.
Nor useless to thy pleasures, happy prince,
Shall be my faithful service; nicer joys,
Joys of a quicker, more exalted taste,

Than

Than ever ripen'd in this northern clime,
The growth of softer regions, shall my hand
By skilful culture in thy Britain raise.
  To them, whose gross and dull capacities
Are fit to bear the burthens of the state,
The lab'ring mules, that through the mire of forms
Draw the slow car of government along,
Gladly the task of bus'ness I resign.
Be mine the brighter province, to direct
Thy pleasures, Edward, minister supreme
Of all thy softer hours; to serve the king
Be theirs the glory, let me serve the man.
  But should thy sterner Genius, only pleas'd
With arms and royalty's important cares,
The duties of a king, my gentle arts
Too lightly prize, and thence reject my suit:
Permit at least, that to Philippa's ear,
Divine Philippa, thine and beauty's queen,
And her attendant graces, I may plead
The cause of bliss, a cause so much their own:
They will approve my claim, to whom the cares,
The labours of my life, my head, my heart
Are all devoted—Let me from their hands
Receive the GARTER, and be call'd their knight.

              PHILIPPA.
  Permit me, gracious Edward, to reply
To this irreverent flatt'rer, who presumes
Before a matron and a queen to plead

                                  The

The cause of vice, and impudently hopes
To find in her a fautress of his suit.
But know, pernicious sophister, my heart
Hath learn'd from Edward's love, and this high rank
Which I partake with him, a noble pride,
That ill can brook the too familiar eye
And saucy tongue of riot and debauch;
In whose unmanner'd light society,
Nor majesty, nor virtue can maintain
That dignity, which is their proper guard.

Thy vile refinements, and luxurious arts,
Miscall'd politeness, I detest; and feel,
In the soft duties of a virtuous love,
Such pure, serene delight, as far transcends
What thou styl'st pleasure, the delirious joy
Of an intoxicated feverish brain.
Behold my royal lord, the first and best
Of kings, the love and wonder of mankind!
Behold my children, worthy their great sire,
The gen'ral theme of praise and benediction!
These are my pleasures; can thy skill bestow
Superior bliss? Ah no, the vain attempt
Would only bring disgust, remorse, and shame.

EDWARD.

That I have lov'd, Philippa, and esteem'd thee
More for thy virtues than those female charms,
Which this vile flatt'rer deems singly worth

His panegyric, be thy happiness
And glory, as it is thy Edward's pride.
  With the like spirit have I also woo'd
And wedded sov'reign pow'r: not weakly caught
With outward pomp, or seeking to myself
A privilege to riot uncontroul'd
In sensual pleasures, and behind the throne
To laugh securely at restraint and law.
No: I embrac'd her as the child of heav'n,
Dow'r'd with the ample means of doing good;
From whose espousals I might hope to raise
An offspring, worth th' ambition of a king,
Immortal glory; to a gen'rous mind
As far surpassing all the wanton toys,
Which he calls pleasure, as thy faithful love
(The sweet o'erflowing of heart-felt delight)
Excels, Philippa, the lascivious smile
Of common prostitutes, caress'd and loath'd.
  Hence from my sight with thy detested arts,
Base minister of luxury, the bane
Of every flourishing and happy state:
Presume no more within my court to sing
Thy Syren-song, nor soften into slaves
And cowards my brave subjects.—I disdain
That elegance, which such as thou can teach.
Virtue alone is elegant, alone
Polite; vice must be sordid and deform'd,
Though to adorn her every art contend.

                              And

And rather would I see my Britons roam
Untutor'd savages, among the woods,
As once they did, in naked innocence,
Than polish'd like the vile degenerate race
Of modern Italy's corrupted sons.

[*Exit* Neap.

Trumpet sounds, and is answered from without by another trumpet, which sounds a march, accompanied by kettle-drums, and other warlike instruments: Then enters, preceded by soldiers playing upon fifes, and others bearing tatter'd ensigns, standards and trophies, a leader of mercenary bands, compleatly arm'd from head to foot, and carrying in his right hand a baton or truncheon. On each side of him march his 'squires, one bearing his lance, the other his shield. Behind him, as his attendants, comes a train of officers and soldiers maimed, and their faces all seam'd with scars.

SOLDIER.

Nor riches, nor nobility of birth,
Nor the soft arts of base effem'nate ease,
Which justly thou rejectest, valiant prince,
But thy own darling attribute I boast,
Undaunted courage, try'd in many a field,
In every clime, and under every banner,
That for these forty summers have been wav'd
O'er Europe's plains, by Ilter, Rhine, and Po,
Hungarian and Bohemian, Flemish, French,
Venetian, Spanish, Guelph and Gibbeline:
Whence in just confidence secure I come
This military honour to demand,

Due

Due to my toils and service, to my wounds,
My laurels, and that gen'rous love of glory,
Which without any call, or public cause,
Or private animosity, alone
Rais'd my strong arm, and drew my dreadful sword.
  Wherever Mars his crimson flag display'd,
That was my country, thither swift I bore
My ready valour, and the dauntless band
Of various nations, under my command,
Prepar'd to sell their blood, their limbs, their lives:
Nor where the right, nor where the justest cause
Deign'd we to ask —— those intricate debates
We left to lazy penmen in the shade
Of coward ease; while our impetuous fire
Still bore us forward, ardent to pursue
Through danger's roughest paths the steps to fame.
On such a spirit should thy favour smile.
  But let me wonder, Edward, that so long
Thy ear the vain pretensions could endure
Of men unknown to war, attendants meet
Of some luxurious Asiatic court,
Or female distaff-reign; but suiting ill
The presence of a monarch great in arms.
Hadst thou to those inglorious sons of peace
Thy martial order giv'n, the warrior-saint
Had blush'd to see his image so profan'd,
Which on my manly breast, indented o'er
With many a noble scar, will fitly shine.

But wherefore ſtand I thus haranguing here,
Unſkilful as I am in ſmooth difcourſe,
The coward's argument? On force alone
I reſt my title: let the glorious prize
Be hung on high amid the liſted field,
And let me there difpute it; there my lance
Shall plead my cauſe far better than my tongue,
If any dare deny my rightful claim.

EDWARD.

Not for the brave alone have I ordain'd
This inſtitution, but for all deſert,
All public virtue, wifdom, all that ſerves,
Improves, defends, or dignifies a ſtate;
Though firſt indeed to valour, as the guard
Of all the reſt, when in the public cauſe,
With juſtice and benevolence employ'd.

But thou, baſe mercenary, canſt thou dare
The glorious name of valour to uſurp,
Who know'ſt no public cauſe, no ſenſe of right,
Nor pity, nor affection, nor remorſe?
Who under any chief, in any quarrel,
Canſt ſtain with gore thy proſtituted arms?
Call it not love of glory; that is built
On acts for the deliv'rance of mankind;
On gen'rous principles, and noble ſcorn
Of ſordid int'reſt: call it cruel pride,
And ſavageneſs of nature, that delights
To conquer, and oppreſs, afflict, inſult;

Or call it love of plunder, that can draw
Unauthoris'd, uninjur'd, unprovok'd,
The sword of war; that bravo-like can lift
For hire the venal hand to perpetrate
Assassinations, murders, massacres.
 But thou hast serv'd with courage: be it so—
Thou hast thy pay, and with it thy reward:
Pretend no farther, nor compare thy deeds,
Dishonour'd by the mean desire of gain,
With his, who for his country and his king
Resigns his ease, his fortune, or his life.
Those battles thou hast fought, those forty years
Of blood and horror, which thy vaunting tongue
So high hath sounded, are indeed thy crimes,
Flagitious crimes; for which th' impartial bar
Of reason would condemn thee, as the foe
Of human nature, did not custom screen
By her unjust esteem thy guilty head.
But hope not honour or employment here.
Unsafe and wretched is that monarch's state
Who weakly trusts to mercenary bands,
The guard or of his person, or his realm;
Unfaithful, insolent, rapacious, base,
He soon shall prove them, and become himself
Their slave, to hold his kingdom at their will.
For this within my Britain have I fought
To raise a martial spirit, and ordain'd
These new incitements, honours, and rewards,

To virtuous chivalry, that never king,
Who wears hereafter my imperial crown,
May need to stoop to the precarious aid
Of venal foreign swords; but in the hearts
Of his brave subjects find a stronger guard,
Prepar'd with zeal unbought, and English valour,
His rights to vindicate, and save their own.
[*Exit* Soldier.

Trumpet sounds, to which another from without replies: Then enters an Italian *politician, habited like a* Venetian *nobleman, who, advancing with a solemn and important air towards the throne, makes a low reverence to king* Edward, *and proceeds.*

POLITICIAN.

Well has thy sovereign wisdom, royal judge,
The suit refus'd of these pretenders vain,
And, by rejecting them, embolden'd me.
For valour, and nobility, and wealth,
Though by their proud possessors vaunted high,
Are but subordinate, the slaves and tools,
Not the companions, and the counsellors
Of godlike monarchy! whose aweful throne
By darksome clouds envelop'd, far beyond
The ken of vulgar eyes, supported stands
On that deep-rooted prop, the craft of state,
Mysterious policy.—Who best hath learn'd
Her wily lessons, best deserves to share

Tha

The honours, counfels, and the hearts of kings.
By him inftructed, ev'n the meaneft prince
Shall rife to envy'd greatnefs, fhall advance
His dreaded pow'r above reftraint and fear,
And all the rules that in fantaftic chains
Inferior minds confine. Thus Milan's dukes,
Thus Padua's lords above their country's laws
Have rais'd their heads, and trampled to the duft
The pride of freedom, that effays in vain
Their high fuperior genius to controul.
Thefe were my mafters, mighty prince; beneath
Their rule, and in their councils was I form'd
To know the falfe corrupted heart of man,
His every weaknefs, every vice, and thence
To tempt, or break his paffions to the yoke:
To fcorn the public as an empty name,
And on the helplefs multitude impofe
The adamantine bonds of fraud and force.
 Thus was I train'd, thus fitted to conduct
The fate of proudeft empires; thus I come
To claim thy GARTER, Edward, the juft meed
Of worth præeminent, and in return
My fervices to offer, which no doubt
Thy wifdom gladly will accept: for who
So fit to ferve the majefty of kings,
As he, who flighting every meaner tye,
Friends, parents, country, to advance their pow'r
Devotes his toil, experience, fortune, fame,

Nor other favour courts, nor refuge hopes
But in their high protection?—Led by me,
Thou, royal Edward, shalt attain that height,
That glorious summit of imperial pow'r,
Which not thy mighty ancestors have reach'd;
Where in a freer air, a more enlarg'd
Horizon, bounded only by thy will,
Thou shalt exalted sit, and view beneath,
In humbler distances and safer bounds,
Those subjects, who presumptuous now approach
Too near, and with rude hands profane thy throne.

 Nor let weak scruples check thy manly soul
In the bright task of glory; know, great prince,
A king's divinity is sov'reign pow'r,
The only god, before whose shrine the wise
Their incense offer, whence inspir'd, they draw
Divine ambition, and heroic scorn
Of vulgar prejudices, vulgar fears.
Virtue's the people's idol, and by them
Rewarded well with popular applause,
That idle breath, the gift and prize of fools.
'Tis thine to govern, not to court mankind,
Nor on their smiles precarious to depend,
But nobly force them to depend on thine.
O sacred sir, can virtue give thee this,
This bright supremacy? Trust not her boasts,
Her idle pageantry of barren praise:
Reject her saucy claims, importunate,

           And

And self-supported; nor admit her train,
Proud independency, and public zeal,
Those factious demagogues, the foes of kings.

    EDWARD.

 Are virtue then, and love of public good,
The foes of monarchy? and are deceit,
Injustice, and oppression, qualities
Becoming and expedient in a king?
Then know I not to govern; but have nurs'd
For twice these fifteen years, ev'n in my heart,
A pois'nous viper; nay unking'd myself,
By yielding to restrain my sov'reign pow'r
With laws and charters of enfranchisement,
Not due, it seems, from monarchs to their slaves.

 But know, vile counsellor of infamy,
That I disdain thy politics, those false
And shallow politics, by which my sire,
Weak-judging Edward, was betray'd to shame
And foul destruction, while to such as thee
His ear and heart incautious he resign'd,
And was indeed their slave, not England's king.

 By maxims different far have I sustain'd
The strength and splendor of my regal state,
On the broad basis of true wisdom fix'd
With solid firmness. By encouraging
The gen'rous love of virtue and of fame,
That source of valour, pledge of victory.

By granting to my subjects, what indeed
Is their inherent right, security,
The cheerful father of content and peace,
Of industry and opulence, which fills
With smiling multitudes the land, and pays
In willing subsidies that prince's care
Who lays up treasure in his people's hearts.

By holding with a firm impartial hand
The steady scale of justice; not alone
Betwixt my subjects in their private rights,
But in the gen'ral, more important cause,
Betwixt the crown and them, the diff'rent claims
Of freedom and of just prerogative;
Transgressing not myself by boundless pow'r,
Nor suff'ring others to transgress those laws,
That in their golden chain together bind,
For common good, the whole united state.

But more than all, by guarding from contempt,
Or impious violation, that supreme
Protectress of all government and law,
Religion; in whose train for ever wait
Obedience, order, justice, mercy, love,
A guard of angels plac'd around the throne.
Her sacred counsels have I still rever'd,
Her high commands enforc'd, her power implor'd,
O'er all my subject nations to call down
From heav'nly wisdom, her eternal fire,

A fix'd

A fix'd secure felicity, beyond
The force of human prudence to attain.
 These are my arts of government, those arts
By which my British crown I have advanc'd
Above th' imperial diadem, above
The pride of Afric's, or of Asia's thrones.
I would not tell thee this, but that thou seem'st
A stranger to my fame, as to my realm,
And to the real greatness of a king:
Whose sacred dignity, by thee traduc'd,
Much it behoves a king to vindicate;
Not by rejecting only with disdain
Thy arrogant pretensions, but in thee
Dishonouring and branding with reproach
Thy tenets also, the pernicious lore
Of tyrants and usurpers, which thy tongue,
Blaspheming justice, government, and law,
Hath in a land of freedom dar'd to vent.
Hence! from my kingdom, with thy quickest speed,
Lest the revenge of an insulted king
With sudden ruin intercept thy flight. [*Exit* Politician.

     King JOHN.
 Permit me, Edward, to thy royal voice
To add my suffrage also, and with thee
Protest against this coward policy,
That meanly skulks behind opprobrious fraud,
And low unprincely artifice; I feel

         A virtue

A virtue in my heart, a gen'rous pride,
That tells me kings were cloath'd with majesty,
Encircled with authority, rever'd
And almost deify'd, to teach them thence
That goodness and the saving attributes
Of heav'n become their office, justice chief,
And truth, the virtue of heroic minds,
Which, were it banish'd from all other breasts,
Should dwell for ever in the hearts of kings.

Aërial music, upon which re-enter the five Druids, *who personated the* Grandee, &c. *in their original characters and habits of* Druids, *the chief of whom advancing towards the throne, addresses himself to king* Edward.

Chief Druid.

Behold in us, great king, the ancient priests
And judges of this land, the Druids old:
Who late in borrow'd characters have stood
Before thy sage tribunal, to prefer
The claims of valour, wealth, nobility,
And those soft specious flatt'rers, who beneath
The rosy wreaths of pleasure and of love
Conceal the sickly and disgustful brow
Of riot and debauch, and often win
From weak unmanly princes the rich prize
To virtue due and wisdom, not to these
The cankers of a state; but least of all
Due to that traytor of his king and country,

Who

Who lab'ring to build up the regal throne
Beyond its due proportion, and the strength
Of those foundations which the laws have laid,
O'erwhelms the people, and at once o'erturns
His royal master, places him at best
On an uneasy tott'ring pinnacle,
The mark of execration and reproach.

 These claims hast thou rejected; like a king
Discerning in mankind, and knowing well
The value of his favours: like a king
Deserving the high office of the judge
And arbiter of Europe: like a king
Equal to his great fame, and worth the care
Of those immortal spirits, who this day
Have quitted their celestial residence,
To view and to approve thy glorious deeds.

 But, Edward, be not thou amaz'd to find
That those who lately for thy favour su'd
Were not the personages they assum'd.
O king! thou art beset with counterfeits
The very oppofites to us, who seem
Far better than they are. For Flattery,
Cameleon-like, accommodates with care
To the court-hue his changeful countenance.
And when a prince is brave, magnanimous,
And high in spirit, then Ambition wears
A face of dignity, and nothing breathes
But lofty enterprizes, conquest, pow'r,

And

And schemes of glory to the sov'reign ear,
Pretending love and care for his renown
With more than duteous zeal —Of these beware!
For as the Theban queen, in fables old,
Was, by the specious guile of fraudful Jove,
In her Amphitryon's form, to guilt betray'd,
So by these counterfeits are kings seduc'd,
Ev'n in the most belov'd suspectless shape,
To take a traytor to their royal arms.
But thou shalt know them, Edward, by their works.
And of this truth be most assur'd, That he,
Who in his private commerce with mankind
Is mean, dishonest, interested, false,
Can ne'er be true to thee; nor can he love
His prince, who feels not for his country's good.

 Thus warn'd we leave thee, mighty prince: be firm,
Be constant in the paths of fair renown.
Think it thy duty to revere thyself
The sacred laws of chivalry, the wise
Injunctions by thy order laid on all
The GARTER'D KNIGHTS; so shall thy fame remain
The great example of all future kings.
Farewell! for lo! the Genius of thy realm,
With all his pomp attended, comes to share,
And grace the glories of this signal day.
These clouds of fragrance, that far-beaming blaze
Of heav'nly brightness, his approach declare.
       [Druids *vanish.*
        Flashes

Flashes of light, and symphony of aërial music. Genius *of* England *descends in his chariot attended by spirits and bards; then alighting, he advances towards the throne, and addresses himself to* Edward.

GENIUS.

From the gay realms of cloudless day I come,
Where in the glitter of unnumber'd worlds,
That like to isles of various magnitudes
Float in the ocean of unbounded space;
On my invisible aërial throne
I sit, attended with a radiant band
Of spirits immortal, whose pure essences,
While clad in human shapes on earth they dwelt,
Through the dull clay of gross mortality
Disclos'd their heav'nly vigour, and burst forth
In godlike virtues and heroic deeds,
Their Albion gracing with as fair a growth
Of fame, as e'er enrich'd imperial Rome.
Thence ripe for heav'n and immortality,
To me, the Genius of this happy isle,
They fly, and claim the meed of their desert,
Celestial crowns, and ever-living praise
Recorded in the songs of heav'nly bards,
That round my throne their hymns of triumph sing,
Attuning to the sweet harmonious spheres
Their undiscording lyres and voice divine.
   Nor thus remov'd to heav'n, and thus employ'd
In ceaseless raptures, wont they to forget

Their

Their native country, and the public weal,
To which on earth their labours and their lives
They once devoted; but purfuing ftill
The bent and habit of their fouls, with me
They watch the Britifh empire, ftill intent
To check alternately th' incroaching waves
Of regal pow'r and popular liberty:
I, chief attentive near the royal throne,
Take up my watchful ftation, to infufe
My fage and mod'rate counfels in thofe ears,
Which wifdom hath prepar'd and purify'd
To relifh honeft, though unpleafing truth.

 Thus am I always, though invifible,
Attendant, Edward, on thy glorious deeds.
But on this folemn day have I vouchfaf'd
To manifeft my prefence; to declare,
Not in thofe whifpers which have often fpoke
Peace to thy confcious heart, but audibly
And evident to all, th' affent of heav'n
To the great bufinefs, which hath gather'd here
This troop of princes from all nations round.
Hence all may know that virtue hath a train
More bright than earthly empire can command:
Know, that thofe actions which are great and good,
Receive a nobler fanction from the free
And univerfal voice of all mankind,
Which is the voice of heav'n, than from the higheft,
The moft illuftrious act of regal pow'r.

            This

This nobler sanction, Edward, in the name
Not of this age alone, but latest time,
Here do I solemnly annex to each
Of thy great acts, but chief to this most wise,
Most virtuous institution, which extends
Wide as thy fame, beyond thy empire's bound,
A prize of virtue publish'd to mankind.
Ye registers of heav'n, record the deed.

BARDS.

Now tune, ye bards, the British lyre;
   Now wake the vocal string;
While heav'n and earth in Edward's praise conspire,
Join to the gen'ral voice your sacred choir,
   And on your soaring wing,
From time and envy waft his glorious name,
And place it in the shrine of incorruptive fame.
   Begin: the list'ning echoes round
   Shall catch with joy the long-forgotten sound,
   And warbling through each grove the British strain
To Windsor's smiling nymphs, recall their Arthur's reign.

   Ye nymphs of Windsor's bow'ry woods,
   Ye pow'rs who haunt yon glist'ning floods,
   That with reluctant fond delay
   Around yon flow'ry valley stray;
   Say, from your minds hath time eras'd
The pleasing images of glory pass'd?

Review

Review ye now those scenes no more;
When nobly stain'd with Saxon gore,
^c From Badon's long-contended plain
Great Arthur with his martial train
To Windsor's chosen shades repair'd,
And with his knights the festive banquet shar'd?

Then first exulting Thames beheld
The triumphs of the listed field;
Beheld along his level meads
Careering knights, encount'ring steeds,
Heroic games, whose toils inspire
The thirst of praise, and kindle martial fire.

Fair Peace in War's bright mail array'd,
With smiles the glorious lists survey'd;
So should the brave (she cry'd) prepare
Their hearts and sinewy arms for war:
Such combats break not my repose,
Such sons best guard my rights from daring foes.

Then too in feastful hall or bow'r,
Attendant on the genial hour,
The British harp sweet lyrists strung,
And Albion's gen'rous victors sung:
While valiant Arthur's copious fame
Incessant fed the bright poetic flame.

^c See Geoffry of Monmouth, B. ix. c. 3.

But mortals erring in excess,
O'erwhelm the virtue they caress.
Thus Arthur his great story mourn'd,
By too fond praise to fable turn'd:
Mourn'd the companions of his toils,
Mock'd with false glory and fantastic spoils.

'Till through the dark romantic tale,
Through superstition's magic veil,
Sage Edward piercing view'd, and own'd
The chief with genuine lustre crown'd:
View'd the great model, and restor'd
The long-lost honours of his martial board.

 Hail British prince! these faithful lays,
 Eternal records of heroic worth,
 Shall reassert thy ancient praise,
 And from the cloud of fiction call thee forth,
 In glory's sphere thy orbit to reclaim,
And at great Edward's beam relume thy darken'd fame.

But see in heav'nly panoply array'd,
 Whose streaming radiance skirts the clouds with gold,
I view Pendragon burst the veiling shade,
 And all his blazing magnitude unfold!
O'er yon broad tow'r he takes his airy stand,
 And pointing, Edward, towards the royal throne,
To his fam'd knights around, a laurel'd band,
Shews on thy knee the bright sky-tinctur'd zone.

Virtue, he cries, (th' æthereal found
Thy grofs material organ cannot hear)
Virtue on earth by Britifh Edward crown'd,
   Her rev'rend throne once more fhall rear.

To her own felf-applauding breaft
Forc'd for reward no longer to retreat,
She fees her awful charms by kings carefs'd,
   Sees honour woo her for his mate.

Honour, her heav'n-elected fpoufe,
From her embrace by lawlefs pow'r with-held,
Now at yon altar plights his holy vows,
   Vows by affenting Edward feal'd.

And now the fair **angelic** bride
Gath'ring her noble train from ev'ry land,
To her late wedded lord with decent pride
   Prefents the venerable band.

The great proceffion Edward leads;
I fee yon hallow'd dome with heroes throng'd:
Inceffant ftill the white-plum'd pomp proceeds,
   Through time's eternal courfe prolong'd.

And you, dear partners of my fame,
Your ancient honours now again fhall boaft;
This noble ORDER fhall retrieve our name,
   In vifionary fables loft.

                                      This

This from our martial board deriv'd,
Thefe for our brethren let us proudly own,
More pleas'd to view our deeds by thee reviv'd,
Than griev'd, great king, to be outdone.

Chorus.

Hail Britifh prince! thefe faithful lays
Shall reaffert thy ancient praife.
Nor thee, O Windfor, fhall I pafs unfung,
Manfion of princes, and fit haunt of gods,
Who frequent fhall defert their bright abodes,
To view thy facred walls with trophies hung;
Thy walls by Britifh Arthur firft renown'd,
The early feat of chivalry and fame;
By Edward now with deathlefs honours crown'd,
Illuftrious by his BIRTH, his GARTER, and his NAME.

Genius.

Conferring juft rewards, moft worthy prince,
Is the firft attribute of fov'reign pow'r,
And that which beft diftinguifhes a king:
For punifhment, and all the nice awards
Of civil juftice, by the laws are fix'd,
And kings but execute what they decree.
While in rewarding merit, uncontroul'd,
Unguided, unaffifted is the hand
Of majefty; the prince himfelf alone
There judges, and his wifdom is the law.
Well does thy court, great king, with every worth

And every virtue fill'd, this wisdom shew
In thee transcendent: well hast thou approv'd
Its force in this great trial, which my pow'r
Commanded, in no common ways to prove
Thy royal mind.—But that a father's name
May not restrain thy justice in the choice
Of the first knights-companions of St. GEORGE,
Myself here take upon me to present
A candidate, whom, were he not thy son,
Thou wouldst thyself select from all mankind.
His modesty compels me to declare
That candidate is Edward, prince of Wales.

    Prince EDWARD.

 Inhabitant of heav'n! I not presume
To deprecate or question that high will,
To which it best becomes me to submit.
But, gentle spirit, be propitious to me;
And thou, my gracious liege, if I request
That this illustrious monarch, whose desert
Is equal to the grandeur of his crown,
May stand before me in this list of fame.

    King JOHN.

 O generous youth! in vain thy goodness strives
To raise thy captive thus above his fortune.
The king that is not free, is not a king;
Nor can thy bounteous favour reconcile
Honour and bondage.—To thy conqu'ring son
Do thou, great Edward, give this noble mark

Of prosp'rous virtue; ill becomes it me,
To wear at once thy GARTER and thy chains.
Though by my former dignity I swear,
That were I reinstated in my throne,
The throne of Capet and of Charlemagne,
Thus to be join'd in fellowship with thee,
Would be the first ambition of my soul;
A ray of glory I would sue to gain,
And prize it equal with my diadem.

    GENIUS.

 Wisely thou hast determin'd, worthy prince,
For thine and Edward's honour, and hast fix'd
Its proper value on his royal gift,
Which, as the meed of merit, may become
The proudest monarchs, by this GARTER mark'd
For something more than monarchs, virtuous men.
This be the glory of thy order, Edward.
And ^c never shall it want the greatest names
Of all succeeding times to grace its annals.
France, Sweden, Poland, Germany, and Spain,
Each realm of Europe's wide-extended bounds,
Shall count among thy knights its mightiest lords,
And see, in emulation of thy fame,

---

 ^c Besides the great persons of our own nation, that have been admitted of this order, the English reader may be glad to be informed, that in the annals of the Garter are found the names of Charles V. emperor of Germany; of Francis I. and Henry IV. kings of France; and of Gustavus Adolphus king of Sweden.

New royal founders of like orders rise.
Proceed then, mighty king, and set the world
The precedent of glory: thou begin
The radiant list of Sovereigns, while thy son,
Like a young bride, that on her nuptial morn
Leads on with modest pride the virgin-choir,
Herself the brightest, heads the shining band
Of knights-companions, nobly seconding
His father's glorious deeds with equal fame.

EDWARD.

The testimony of heav'n to thee, my son,
Thus gloriously accorded, renders vain
All farther trial.—To my people's voice,
By this their tutelary pow'r declar'd,
With pleasure I consent, directing still
By theirs my choice, my judgment, my desires.

Approach then, my belov'd, my noble son,
Strength of my crown, and honour of my realm;
In whom my heart more joys, and glories more,
Than in the highest pride of sov'reign pow'r.

^d Thus I admit thee, Edward prince of Wales,
First founder of the order of St. GEORGE:
In evidence whereof, about thy knee
I bind this mystic GARTER; to denote
The bond of honour that together ties

---

^d The prince of Wales advances to his father, and kneels; while the king, taking the Garter from the herald, buckles it round his left leg.

The brethren of St. GEORGE in friendly league,
United to maintain the cause of truth
And justice only— ᵉ " May propitious heav'n
" Grant thou may'st henceforth wear it to his praise,
" The exaltation of this noble order,
" And thy own glory."—With like reverence,
My son, receive and wear this golden chain,
" Grac'd with the image of Britannia's saint,
" Heav'n's valiant soldier, CAPPADOCIAN GEORGE;
" In imitation of whose glorious deeds
" May'st thou triumphant in each state of life,
" Or prosperous or adverse, still subdue
" Thy spiritual and carnal enemies;
" That not on earth alone thou may'st obtain
" The guerdon of thy valour, endless praise,
" But with the virtuous and the brave above,
" In solemn triumph, wear celestial palms,
" To crown thy final noblest victory."
        [*Embraces Pr.* EDW.
    Prince EDWARD.
Accept, my sov'reign liege, my grateful thanks,
That thou hast thus vouchsaf'd to place thy son
First next thyself upon the roll of fame,

ᵉ The sense, and almost the words in the verses of this speech, mark'd thus " are taken from the admonition read to the knights, at the time of their receiving the GARTER and the RIBBON or COLLAR of the order. Vide Ashmole's History of the order of the GARTER.

As he indeed is first in filial love,
And emulation of thy royal virtues.
And may thy benediction, gracious lord,
May thy paternal vows be heard in heav'n!
That he, whom thou hast lifted in the cause
Of truth and virtue, never may forget
His vow'd engagements, nor defraud thy hopes,
By soiling with dishonourable deeds
The lustre of that ORDER, which thy name
Should teach him to respect and to adorn.

ODE.
STROPHE I. BARDS.

   Celestial maid!
 Bright spark of that æthereal flame,
Whose vivid spirit through all nature spread,
Sustains and actuates this boundless frame!
O by whatever stile to mortals known,
Virtue, benevolence, or public zeal,
Divine assessor of the regal throne,
Divine protectress of the common weal,
O in our hearts thy energy infuse!
   Be thou our Muse,
   Celestial maid,
And, as of old, impart thy heav'nly aid
To those, who, warm'd by thy benignant fire,
To public merit and their country's good
Devoted ever their recording lyre,
Wont along DEVA's sacred flood,

Or,

Or, beneath Mona's oak retir'd,
To warble forth their patriot lays,
And nourish with immortal praise
The bright heroic flames by thee inspir'd.

ANTISTROPHE I.

I feel, I feel
Thy soul-invigorating heat;
My bounding veins distend with fervent zeal,
And to Britannia's fame responsive beat.―――
Hail Albion, native country! but how chang'd
Thy once grim aspect, how adorn'd and gay
Thy howling forests! where together rang'd
The naked hunter and his savage prey;
Where amid black inhospitable woods
  The sedge-grown floods
  All cheerless stray'd,
Nor in their lonely wand'ring course survey'd
Or tow'r, or castle, heav'n-ascending fane,
Or lowly village, residence of peace
And joyous industry, or furrow'd plain,
  Or lowing herd, or silver fleece
  That whitens now each verdant vale;
  While laden with their precious store
  Far trading barks to every shore,
Swift heralds of Britannia's glory, sail.

EPODE

EPODE I.

These are thy shining works: this smiling face
Of beauteous nature thus in regal state,
Deck'd by each handmaid art, each polish'd grace,
That on fair liberty and order wait.
  This pomp, these riches, this repose,
  To thee imperial Britain owes.
To thee, great substitute of heav'n,
To whom the charge of earthly realms was giv'n;
Their social systems by wise nature's plan
To form and rule by her eternal laws;
To teach the selfish soul of wayward man
To seek the public good, and aid the common cause.
  So didst thou move the mighty heart
Of Alfred, founder of the British state:
  So to Matilda's ᶠ scepter'd son,
  To him whose virtue and renown
  First made the name of Edward great,
Thy ample spirit so didst thou impart:
  Protecting thus in every age,
  From greedy pow'r and factious rage,
That law of freedom, which to Britain's shore
From Saxon Elva's many-headed flood,
The valiant sons of Odin with them bore,
Their national, ador'd, inseparable good.

   ᶠ Henry IId.

STROPHE

STROPHE II.

^g On yonder plain,
Along whose willow-fringed side
The silver-footed Naiads, sportive train,
Down the smooth Thames amid the cygnets glide,
I saw, when, at thy reconciling word,
Injustice, anarchy, intestine jar,
Despotic insolence, the wasting sword,
And all the brazen throats of civil war,
Were hush'd in peace; from his imperious throne
    Hurl'd furious down,
    Abash'd, dismay'd,
Like a chas'd lion to the savage shade
Of his own forests, fell oppression fled,
With vengeance brooding in his sullen breast.
Then Justice fearless rear'd her decent head,
    Heal'd every grief, each wrong redress'd;
    While round her valiant squadrons stood,
    And bade her awful tongue demand,
    From vanquish'd John's reluctant hand,
The deed of freedom purchas'd with their blood.

^g Runny Mead near Stains, where the Grand Charter was signed by king John.

ANTISTROPHE II.

O vain surmise!
To deem the grandeur of a crown
Consists in lawless pow'r! to deem them wise
Who change security and fair renown,
For detestation, shame, distrust, and fear!
Who, shut for ever from the blissful bow'rs,
With horror and remorse at distance hear
The music that inchants th' immortal pow'rs,
The heav'nly music of well-purchas'd praise,
    Seraphic lays,
      The sweet reward
On heroes, patriots, righteous kings conferr'd.
For such alone the heav'n-taught poets sing.
Tune ye for Edward, then, the mortal strain,
His name shall well become your golden string;
    Begirt with this æthereal train,
    Seems he not rank'd among the gods?
    Then let him reap the glorious meed
    Due to each great heroic deed,
And taste the pleasures of the blest abodes.

EPODE II.

Hail, happy prince! on whom kind Fate bestows
    Sublimer joys, and glory brighter far
    Than Cressy's palm, and every wreath that grows
    In all the blood-stain'd field of prosp'rous war;

Joys that might charm an heav'nly breast,
To make dependent millions blest,
A dying nation to restore,
And save fall'n liberty with kingly pow'r;
To quench the torch of discord and debate,
Relume the languid spark of public zeal,
Repair the breaches of a shatter'd state,
And gloriously compleat the plan of England's weal;
Complete the noble Gothic pile,
That on the rock of justice rear'd shall stand
In symmetry, and strength, and fame,
A rival of that boasted frame
Which virtue rais'd on Tiber's strand.
This, Edward, guardian, father of our isle,
This god-like task, to few assign'd,
Exalts thee above human-kind.
And from the realms of everlasting day
Calls down celestial bards thy praise to sing;
Calls this bright troop of spirits to survey
Thee, the great miracle of earth, a PATRIOT-King.

GENIUS.

Now reascend your skies, immortal spirits!
Th' important act, that drew ye down to earth,
Is finish'd. Spare we now their mortal sense,
That cannot long endure th' unshrouded beam
Of higher natures. Well hath Edward laid,
Under your happy auspices, the base
Of his great ORDER: let him undisturb'd,

But

But not unaided by the heav'nly powers,
Complete th' illustrious work, which future kings,
Struck with the beauty of the noble plan,
Shall emulously labour to maintain.
 And may thy spirit, Edward, be their guide!
In every chapter, thou henceforth preside,
In every breast infuse thy virtuous flame,
And teach them to respect their country's fame.
   [*Genius and* Spirits *reascend to a loud*
      symphony of music.

An Epistle to the Right Honourable the Lord Viscount CORNBURY.

By ———, Esq;

WHILE you, my Lord, alas! amidst a few,
 With generous warmth your country's good pursue;
While to that centre all your wishes tend,
Accept the zeal that prompts a willing friend.
 Others like you heav'n's hallow'd spark inspir'd,
Whom soon the blaze of selfish passion fir'd,
Soon ruder flames extinguish'd reason's light,
While prejudices foul'd their jaundiced sight.
 Such through false optics every object prove,
And try the good and bad, by hate and love.

All-powerful means each virtue to supply,
All-powerful means each virtue to deny;
To Wyndham [h] strength, and grace, and fire, and weight;
To Granville [i] parts, to save a sinking state.
Hence various judgments form the madden'd throng,
Only in this alike, they all are wrong.
Hence to false praise shall blame unjust succeed,
And cherubs fall, and gods unpity'd bleed.

   Would you, my friend, not mix the purer flame,
Nor lose the patriot in a baser name;
Nor factious rage mistake for public zeal,
Nor private int'rest for the gen'ral weal?
By truth's sure test let every deed be try'd,
And justice ever be th' unerring guide.
Her rules are plain, and easy is her way,
And yet how hard to find if once we stray!
All lost alike the maze perplex'd we tread,
However prompted, whether drove or led;
Whether false honour or ambition goad,
Or sneaking av'rice wind the miry road,
Or whether sway'd by passion's not our own,
And the weak fear of being right alone.
Alone in such a cause 'tis base to fear,
Though fools suspect, and knaves designing sneer.
Sneer, villains, sneer! th' avenging time is nigh,
When Balbo scourg'd shall weep the taunting lie;
When Stopus foul with each imputed crime,
Shall dread false prose repaid with honest rhyme.

[h] Sir William Wyndham.   [i] John earl of Granville.

'Tis

'Tis not enough you scorn a private claim,
And to your country's good direct your aim.
Wrong is still wrong, however great the end,
Though all the realm were brother, father, friend;
Justice regards not these——where right prevails,
A nation is an atom in her scales.
Heaven means not all the good which man can gain,
But that which truth can earn, and right maintain.
However fair the tempting prize may be,
If guilt the price, it is not meant for thee.
Succeeding times may claim the just design,
Or other means, or other powers than thine.

 Each part's connected with the gen'ral plan,
The weal of Britain, with the weal of man.
Justice the scale of interest for the whole,
The same in Indies as beneath the pole;
Sure rule by which heav'n's blessings to dispense,
Unerring light of guiding providence.
Others may fail.——If wrongly understood,
How fatal is the thirst of public good !
No heavier curse almighty vengeance brings,
Nor plagues, nor famine, nor the lust of kings.
Fir'd by this rage, the frantic sons of Rome,
The suff'ring world to death and bondage doom;
Nations must sink to raise her cumb'rous frame,
And millions bleed to eternize her name.
But lo ! her glories fade, her empire's past,
She madly conquer'd but to fall the last.

Nor

Nor would I here the patriot's views reprove;
Or damp the sacred flame of social love;
Still may that portion of th' eternal ray
Sublime our sense, and animate our clay;
Above low self exalt th' immortal frame,
And emulate that heav'n from whence it came.
Oh! would it never be confin'd to place,
But beam extensive as the human race:
Be, as it was design'd, the world's great soul,
Connect its parts, and actuate the whole.
So each should think himself a part alone,
And for a nation's welfare stake his own!
Yet farther still, though dearest to the breast,
That nation think but part of all the rest.

For this let equal justice poise the ball,
Her swaying force unites us all to all;
Of manners, worship, form, no diff'rence knows,
Condemns our friends, and saves our better foes.
Confess the heavenly power! nor need you fear
Lest Britain suffer, while you follow her.

Though prosp'rous crimes some daring villains raise,
Nor life's short date may halting vengeance seize;
A nation cannot 'scape——the destin'd rage
Pursues her ceaseless to some future age;
Speeds the sure ruin from the conqueror's hand,
Or spreads corruption o'er a pining land.

Ask hoary Time, what nation is most blest?
For sage experience shall this truth attest:

" Where

" Where freedom sleeps secure from lawless wrath,
" Where commerce shelter'd flows through public faith,
" Where fell ambition lights no foreign wars,
" Nor discord rages with intestine jars;
" Where justice reigns."—Immortal were that state,
If aught immortal here were giv'n by Fate.

    Such, lost Iberia! were those happy reigns,
When liberty sat brooding o'er thy plains.
The rich in plenteous peace their stores enjoy'd,
By cares unvex'd, by luxury uncloy'd.
Hope sooth'd the poor with promises of gain,
And paid with future joys their present pain;
Shew'd the full bowl amidst their sultry toil,
While those who prun'd the olive drank the oil;
By night of all the fruits of day possest,
Labour soft-clos'd the eye, and sweeten'd rest.
Such was thy state, all gay in nature's smiles!
And such is now the state of Britain's isles.
Hence o'er the ocean's waste her sail unfurl'd,
Wide wafts the tribute of a willing world.
Hence trusting nations treasure here their wealth,
Safe from tyrannic force or legal stealth:
And hence the injur'd exile doom'd to roam,
Shall find his country here and dearer home.

    Still be this truth, this saving truth confest,
Britain is great, because with freedom blest;
Her prince is great, because her people free,
And power here springs from public liberty.

Hail

Hail mighty monarch of the free and great!
Firm on the basis of a prosp'rous state.
The wealth, the strength of happy millions thine,
United rise, united shall decline,
For time will come, sad period of the brave,
When Britain's humble prince shall rule the slave;
When traffic vile shall stain the guilty throne,
And kings shall buy our ruin and their own.
 But long, O long th' inglorious doom suspend!
What virtue gain'd may virtue still defend!
Thrice sacred spirit, never may you cease,
But as you blaz'd in war, shine forth in peace!
Dauntless with all the force of truth engage
The headlong tide of each corrupted age.
O ever wake around one favour'd throne,
Nor let our guardian monarch wake alone!
 Though oft defeated, and though oft betray'd,
Numbers shall rise in sacred freedom's aid.
Far as her all-enlivening influence reigns,
Heroic ardour beats in gen'rous veins;
Now bids learn'd Greece barbarian might defy,
Now the soft arts of polish'd tyranny;
Now to no stock, or sect, or place confin'd,
She takes adopted sons from human kind;
While denizen'd by her eternal laws,
They all are Britons who shall serve her cause.
 Lo! to the banner crowds a youthful band;
Form'd for the glorious task by nature's hand;

M 2   Wisdom

Wisdom unclogg'd by years, with toil unbought,
A zeal by vigour kindled, rul'd by thought.
Such gifts she to the happy few imparts,
To judging heads and to determin'd hearts;
To heads unfir'd by youth's tumultuous rage,
To hearts unnumb'd by the chill ice of age;
And while they both preserve a sep'rate claim,
Their passions reason, and their reasons flame,

    Proceed, brave youths! Let others court renown
In hostile fields, be yours the olive crown:
And trust to fame, those heroes brighter shone
Who sav'd a nation, than who nations won.
Nor let assuming age restrain your flight,
Fearful to tempt the yet unpractis'd height;
Deceitful counsel lurks in hoary hairs,
And the last dregs of life are sordid cares.

    Objects are clear proportion'd in degree,
To gen'ral use, or strong necessity.
Nor are two things so plainly understood,
As the worst evil, and the greatest good;
If, rescu'd from the misty breath of schools,
Men will but feel without the help of rules.
So unbewilder'd in the crooked maze,
Where guilt low sculks, and reptile cunning strays,
A nation's interest, and a people's rights,
Distinctly shine in nature's simple lights,
And claim in him who fairly acts his part,
Before a Lonsdale's head, a Lonsdale's heart.

But

But chief when fnatch'd by heaven's preferving hand,
From the fell contefts of each hoftile land,
A happy ifland to th' incircling main
Trufts for a fure fupport and honeft gain.

   The juft are heaven's, earth is for heaven ordain'd,
Form'd by its laws, and by its laws maintain'd.
Thefe one true int'reft, one great fyftem frame,
Political and moral are the fame.
Guilt toils for gain at honour's vaft expence,
Heaven throws the trifle in to innocence;
And fixes happinefs in hell's defpite,
The neceffary confequence of right.

   Proceed, ye Deifts! blindfold rage employ,
And prove the facred truths you would deftroy.
Prove Chriftian faith the wifeft fcheme to bind,
In chains of cordial love, our jarring kind;
And thence conclude it human, if you can,
The perfect produce of imperfect man!
While proftrate we adore that power divine,
Whofe fimple rule connects each great defign;
Bids focial earth a type of heaven appear,
Where juftice taftes thofe joys which wait her there.

   But though felf-int'reft follow virtue's train!
Yet felfifh think not virtue's end is gain!
Older than time, ere int'reft had a name,
Juftice exifted, and is ftill the fame;
Alike the creature's and creator's guide,
His rule to form, the law by which we're ty'd:

In reason's light, eternal word, exprest,
Stamp'd with his image in the creature's breast.
   Thus speaks the sage, who skill'd in nature's laws,
Deep from effects high-trac'd th' all-ruling cause.
" Before creation was, th' Almighty Mind
" In time's abyss the future world design'd;
" Did the great system in its parts survey,
" And fit the springs, and regulate their play;
" In meet gradations plann'd th' harmonious round,
" These links by which depending parts are bound.
" All these he knew, ere yet the things he made,
" In types which well the mimic world display'd.
" The types are real, since from them he drew
" The real forms of whatsoe'er we view,
" Made to their 'semblance, heav'n and earth exist,
" But they unmade eternally subsist.
" For if created, we must sure suppose
" Some other types whence their resemblance flows;
" While these on others equally depend,
" Nor ever shall the long progression end.
" God ere it was, the future being saw,
" Or blindfold made his world, and gave his law.
" But chance could never frame the vast design,
" Where countless parts in justest order join,
  " The types eternal just proportions teach,
" Greater or less, more or less perfect each.
" These ever present power omiscient sees,
" On them he forms his ever-made decrees;

" Nor

" Nor can he better love what merits least,
" Man than an angel, or than man a beast.
" Hence Reason, hence immortal Order springs,
" Knowledge and Love adapted to the things.
" And thence th' unerring rule of justice flows,
" To act what Order prompts, and Reason shows.
　" When man in nature's purity remain'd,
" By pain untroubled, and by sin unstain'd;
" Fair image of the God, and close conjoin'd,
" By innate union with the heav'nly mind;
" In the pure splendor of substantial light,
" The beam divine of Reason bless'd his sight;
" Seraphic order in its fount he view'd,
" Seeing he lov'd, and loving he pursu'd;
" Nor dar'd the body, passive slave, controul
" The sov'reign mandates of the ruling soul.
" But soon by sin the sacred union broke,
" Man bows to earth beneath the heavy yoke.
" The darkling soul scarce feels a glimm'ring ray,
" Shrouded in sense from her immortal day.
" Vengeance divine offended Order arms,
" And clothes in terrors her celestial charms.
" Now grosser objects heav'n-born souls possess,
" Passions enslave, and servile cares oppress.
" Fraud, rapine, murder, guilt's long horrid train,
" Distracted nature's anarchy maintain.
" No more pure Reason earthly minds can move,
" No more can Order's charms persuasive prove.

"

" But as the moon reflecting borrow'd day,
" Sheds on our shadow'd world a feeble ray;
" Some scatter'd beams of Reason law contains,
" While Order's rule must be enforc'd by pains.
" Hence death's black scroll, dire tortures hence are giv'n;
" Hence kings, the necessary curse of heav'n.
" And just the doom of an avenging God,
" Who spurn'd his sceptre, feel the tyrant's rod.
" Blind by our fears we meet the ills we fly,
" In rule oppression, want in property."
So spoke the sage, and if not learn'd in vain,
If spotless truth in sacred books remain ;
Dearly the child hath paid the parent's pride,
And ill hath Law the heavenly rule supply'd.
Thus boasts some leech with unavailing art,
To mend the tainted lungs and wasting heart ;
Bids the loose springs with wonted vigour play,
And sprightly juices warm in cold decay.

Or would imperious reason deign to own,
The world not made for sovereign man alone ;
Some things there are for human use design'd,
And these in common dealt to human kind.
To mortal wants is given a power to use,
What to th' immortal part just heav'n might well refuse,
This faithful instinct in each breast implants,
All know their rights, for all must feel their wants.

But soon began the rage of wild desire
To thirst for more than use could e'er require.

Ere

Ere stung by luxury's unsated call,
And ere ambition madly grasp'd the ball,
Vain restless man in busy search employ'd,
Saw somewhat still beyond the bliss enjoy'd,
Press'd eager on; the lowly and the great,
Alike their wish beyond their destin'd state;
Alike condemn'd, whatever Fortune grant,
To real poorness in phantastic want.

And now some sages high by others deem'd,
For virtue honour'd, and for parts esteem'd;
Call'd forth to judge where dubious claims are try'd,
Convince with reason, and with counsel guide;
Fix'd rules devise to sway th' assenting throng,
And marks distinct impress on right and wrong.

The simple precept subtle wiles evade,
And statutes as our crimes increas'd were made:
These were at first unwritten, plain and few,
'Till swell'd by time the law's vast volume grew;
And grown with these, to sway th' unwieldy trust,
Thousands we chose to keep the millions just,
Some plac'd o'er others, others plac'd o'er these,
Thus government grew up by slow degrees;
Higher the pile arose, and still more high,
When lo! the summit ends in monarchy.
There plac'd, a man in gorgeous pomp appears,
And far o'er earth his tow'ring aspect rears;
While prostrate crowds his sacred smiles implore,
And what their crimes had form'd, their fears adore.

Low

Low from beneath they lift their servile eyes,
And see the proud colossus touch the skies.
  So at some mountain's foot have children gaz'd,
While close to heaven they view the summit rais'd,
Eager they mount, new regions to explore,
But heav'n is now as distant as before.
Thus views the crowd a throne, while those who rise
Claim not a nearer kindred to the skies;
Earth is their parent, thither kings should bend,
From thence they rise, and not from heaven descend.
Happy, had all the royal sons of earth
Thus sprung, nor guilt had claim'd the monstrous birth,
Where from the sire descending through the line,
Rapine and fraud confer a right divine.
  Ye mortal gods, how vainly are ye proud?
If just your title, servants to the crowd;
If wide your sway, if large your treasur'd store,
These but increase your servitude the more;
A part is only yours, the rest is theirs,
And nothing all your own, except your cares.
Shall man, by nature free, by nature made
To share the feast her bounteous hand display'd,
Transfer these rights? as well he may dispense
The beam of reason, or the nerve of sense;
With all his strength the monarch's limbs invest,
Or pour his valour in the royal breast.
  Take the starv'd peasant's taste, devouring lord!
Ere you deprive him of the genial board.

And

And if you would his liberty controul,
Assume the various actings of his soul!
So shall one man a people's powers enjoy,
Thus Indians deem of wretches they destroy.
Thus in old tales the fabled monster stands,
Proud of a thousand eyes, a thousand hands.
Thus dreams the sophist, who with subtle art
Would prove the whole included in a part,
A people in their king; and from the throng,
Transfer to him their rights in nature's wrong;
Those sacred rights in nature's charter plain,
By wants that claim them, and by powers that gain.

   Though sophists err, yet stand confess'd thy claim,
And be the king and multitude the same,
Whose deeds benevolent his title prove,
And royal selfishness, in public love;
Nor, draining wasted realms for sordid pelf,
O scepter'd suicide! destroy thyself.

   Where fails this proof, in vain would we unite
The ruler's int'rest with the people's right.
Frantic ambition has her sep'rate claim,
The dropsy'd thirst of empire, wealth, or fame;
Pride's boundless hope, valour's enthusiast rant,
With the long nameless train of fancy'd want.
Urg'd on by these, all view the magic prize,
The prospect widening as they higher rise;
From him who seeks a limited command,
To him whose wish devours air, sea, and land.

Alike

Alike all foes to freedom's holy cause,
For freedom ties unbounded will with laws;
Alike all foes to every public gain,
For public blessings loose the bond-man's chain.
    Ill-fated slaves of arbitrary sway!
Where trusted power seduces to betray;
Makes private failings rage a gen'ral pest,
And taints even virtue in the social breast;
Bids friendship plunder, charity undo
The blameless MANY, for the favour'd FEW.
'Till guilt high rear'd on crimes protecting crime,
Fills the heap'd measure of predestin'd time.
    Far others, ye, O wealthy, wise, and brave!
Though subject, free; more freedom would enslave,
Bless'd with a rule by long experience try'd,
Unwarp'd by faction's rage, or kingly pride;
Bless'd with the means, whene'er this rule shall bend,
Again to trace it to its glorious end;
And bless'd with proofs, the proofs are seal'd with blood,
Whate'er the form, the end is public good.
    But yet admit the sire his right foregoes!
Can he his children's sep'rate claim dispose?
Whate'er the parent gave, whate'er he give,
They who have right to life, have right to live.
And spite of man's consent, or man's decree,
A right to life, is right to liberty.
    Though for convenience fram'd the laws should shine,
Pure emanation from the source divine;

                              Such

Such as can pierce the gloom of pagan night,
And untaught favages in woods enlight;
Such as on fcaffolds can the guiltlefs fave,
And torture on his throne the fcepter'd flave;
Such as th' offending wretch reluctant owns,
And hails its beauty with his dying groans:
In fuch fair laws the will of heav'n imprefs'd,
Shines to all eyes, and rules the confcious breaft.
Though tortures ceafe, though night's thick-mantling vail
From mortal ken the fecret deed conceal;
Reafon and confcience fhall awake within,
And light the fhade, and loud proclaim the fin.

" But fhould the univerfal voice combine,
" To cloath injuftice in a robe divine?"
Let the fame breath diveft the day of light,
To blazon forth the dufky face of night.
Then fhall the laws of fainted evil bind,
And human will fubvert th' all-ruling mind;
That facred fount whence lawful rule muft fpring,
And diff'rent from the robber marks the king.

Yet vainly would defpotic will conclude,
That force may fway the erring multitude,
Juftice, 'tis own'd, fhould ever guide the free,
But pow'r of wrong, in all, is liberty;
And for whatever purpofes reftrain'd,
A nation is enflav'd that may be chain'd.
Heaven gives to all a liberty of choice,
A people's good requires a people's voice;

Man's

Man's surest guide, where diff'rent views agree,
From private hate, and private int'rest free.
Fatal their change from such who rashly fly,
To the hard grasp of guiding tyranny;
Soon shall they find, when will is arm'd with might,
Injustice wield the sword, though drawn for right.

 Blind to these truths who fond of boundless sway,
Bids trembling slaves implicitly obey;
Though by a long descent from Adam down
Through scepter'd heirs, he boasts his ancient crown,
Great nature's rebel forfeits every claim,
And loads the tyrant with th' usurper's name;
While with each lawless act of proud command,
He stands proscrib'd by his own guilty hand.

 Bow, Filmer [k], bow! to hell's tremendous throne,
And bid thy fellow-damn'd suppress each groan!
There sits a king whom pow'r divine hath giv'n,
Nor earth boasts one so surely sent from heav'n.
And thou, blest martyr [l] in fair freedom's cause,
Thou great assertor of thy country's laws;
Vainly oppression stopp'd thy potent breath;
Truth shone more powerful through the vail of death;
Example mov'd whom precept could not save,
And lifted axes wak'd each drowsy slave.

 Yet magistrates must rule, they're useful things,
Our guilt the vengeance, and avenger brings.

---

[k] Sir Robert Filmer, author of "Patriarcha; or, the Natural Power of Kings," and other pieces of the same tendency. He was answered by Mr. Locke, in his Essay on Government.

[l] Algernon Sydney.

What-

Whate'er more perfect heav'n might first create,
A state well govern'd, now, is nature's state;
For law from reason springs, spontaneous fruit,
And reason sure is man's first attribute.
Let visionary schoolmen toil in vain,
Who seek in anarchy for nature's reign;
Wretched alike the slaves of lawless will,
Whether the savage, or the tyrant kill;
Unjust alike all rule, where public choice
Speaks not through laws a willing people's voice.
Nor freedom suffers when the guilty fall,
'Tis nature's doom, 'tis self-defence in all.

   Such now is man deprav'd, that fear must sway
To tread the paths where duty points the way;
The wretch must suffer to forewarn the rest,
And some must fall to stop the spreading pest.
Alone the gen'ral welfare can demand
The bleeding victim from th' unwilling hand.

   Hence public pains—what to the crime is due,
O Judge supreme! must be reserv'd for you.
To you alone, whose all-pervading eye
Deep in the breast can latent thought espy;
Try every action by the known intent,
And to each crime adapt its punishment;
While men, misled by erring lights, dispense
The doom of guilt to injur'd innocence;
Or though repentance cleanse the moral stain,
Inflict on crimes aton'd avenging pain.

                                Yet

Yet blameless they who act sincere their part,
Faultless he errs who cannot read the heart.

 Not such fierce flames the mad enthusiast's zeal,
On errors harmless to the gen'ral weal,
Whether false notions wander far from truth,
Or age retain the trace impress'd in youth.
While int'rest prompts the holy murd'rer's hand,
In sacred fires to light th' unhallow'd brand;
To draw destruction from heaven's saving page,
And bid sweet mercy breathe relentless rage.

 Accurs'd all such! and he with joy elate,
Whose baleful breath embitters certain fate;
Who on th' imploring face malignant smiles,
And sentenc'd wretches wantonly reviles.
Better, far better in the savage den,
Let the robb'd lion judge o'er prostrate men:
Better let pow'r the lawless faulchion draw,
Then coward cruelty disgrace the law.

 This well you know, O —— ! whose righteous seat
Gives to the innocent a sure retreat;
Severely just, and piously humane,
The wretch you punish, while you share his pain.
Tears with the dreadful words of sentence flow,
Nor does the rigid judge the man forego.

 So feels the breast humane, ye truly brave!
And such is thine, my friend, intent to save!
Whether thy bounty pining want relieve,
Or lenient pity sooth the hearts that grieve;

Whether

Whether thy pious hand due bounds prescribe
To little tyrants, o'er the lesser tribe;
Or whether nobler warmth expand thy soul,
And huge leviathan unaw'd controul.
  Nor Britain only claims thy gen'rous plan,
Thy rule is justice, and thy care is man.
And may this truth thy fair example prove,
Justice shall fan the flame of social love.

✣✣✣✣✣✣✣✣✣✣✣✣✣✣✣✣✣✣✣✣✣✣✣✣✣✣✣✣✣✣✣✣

An EPISTLE.
By the Same.

THROUGH the wild maze of life's still varying plan,
  Bliss is alone th' important task of man.
All else is trifling, whether grave or gay,
A Newton's labours, or an infant's play;
Whether this vainly wastes th' unheeded sun,
Or those more vainly mark the course it run;
For of the two, sure smaller is the fault,
To err unthinking, than to err with thought;
But if, like them, we still must trifles use,
Harmless at least, like theirs, be those we chuse.
Enough it is that reason blames the choice,
Join not to her's the wretch's plaintive voice;
Be folly free from guilt: let foplings play,
Or write, or talk, or dress, or die away.
Let those, if such there be, whose giant-mind
Superior tow'rs above their pigmy kind,

Unaided

Unaided and alone, the realms explore,
Where hail and snow renew their treasur'd store *.
Lo! heav'n spreads all its stars; let those explain,
What balanc'd pow'rs the rolling orbs sustain;
Nor in more humble scales, pernicious weigh
Sense, justice, truth, against seducing pay.
So distant regions shall employ their thought,
And spotless senates here remain unbought.

  Well had great † Charles, by early want inspir'd,
With warring puppets, guiltless praise acquir'd;
So would that flame have mimic fights engag'd,
Which fann'd by pow'r, o'er wasted nations rag'd.

  Curs'd be the wretch, should all the mouths of fame,
Wide o'er the world his deathless deeds proclaim,
Who like a baneful comet spreads his blaze,
While trembling crowds in stupid wonder gaze;
Whose potent talents serve his lawless will,
Which turns each Virtue to a public ill,
With direful rage perverted might employs,
And heav'n's great ends with heav'n's best means destroys.
The praise of power is his, whose hand supplies
Fire to the bold, and prudence to the wise;
While man this only real merit knows,
Fitly to use the gifts which heav'n bestows:

---

  * Job, chap. xxxviii.
  † Charles V. Emperor of Germany, who in his retirement amus'd himself with puppets. See Strada de bello Belgico.

If savage valour be his vaunted fame,
The mountain-lion shall dispute his claim :
Or, if perfidious wiles deserve applause,
Through slighted vows, and violated laws ;
The subtle plotter's title stands confess'd,
Whose dagger gores the trusting tyrant's breast.
And sure the villain less deserves his fate,
Who stabs one wretch, than he who stabs a state.
Now, mighty hero ! boast thy dear delights,
The price of toilsome days and sleepless nights ;
Say, canst thou aught in purple grandeur find,
Sweet as the slumbers of the lowly hind ?

 Better are ye, the youthful and the gay,
Who jocund rove through pleasure's flow'ry way !
Yet seek not there for bliss ! your toil were vain,
(And disappointed toil is double pain)
Though from the living fount your nectar-bowls
Pour the soft balm upon your thirsty souls ;
Though pure the spring, though every draught sincere,
By pain unbitter'd, and unpall'd by fear ;
Though all were full as high as thought can soar,
'Till fancy fires, and wishes crave no more :
Let lovely woman artless charms display,
Where truth and goodness bask in beauty's ray ;
Let heav'nly melody luxuriant float
In swelling sounds, and breathe the melting note ;
Let gen'rous wines enliv'ning thoughts inspire,
While social converse sooths the genial fire :

If aught can yet more potent charms difpenfe,
Some ftronger rapture, fome fublimer fenfe;
Be thefe enjoy'd.—Then from the crowd arife
Some chief, in life's full pride maturely wife.
Ev'n you, my Lord, with titles, honours grac'd,
And higher ftill by native merit plac'd;
By ftinted talents to no fphere confin'd;
Free ranging every province of the mind:
Equally fit, a nation's weight to bear,
Or fhine in circles of the young and fair;
In grave debates inftructed fenates move,
Or melt the glowing dame to mutual love.
To heighten thefe, let confcious worth infufe
Sweet eafe, and fmiling mirth th' infpiring Mufe.
Then anfwer, thou of every gift poffefs'd,
Say, from thy foul, art thou fincerely bleft!
To various objects wherefore doft thou range?
Pleafure muft ceafe, ere man can wifh to change.
Haft thou not quitted Flaccus' facred lay,
To talk with Bavius, or with Flavia play;
When wafted nature fhuns the large expence
Of deep attention to exalted fenfe!
Precarious blifs! which foon, which oft muft cloy,
And which how few, how very few enjoy!

 Say, is there aught, on which, completely bleft,
Fearlefs and full the raptur'd mind may reft?
Is there aught conftant? Or, if fuch there be,
Can varying man be pleas'd with conftancy?

Mark

Mark then what sense the blessing must employ!
The senses change, and loath accustom'd joy:
Eden in vain immortal sweets displays,
If the taste sickens, or our frame decays.

   The range of life contracted limits bound;
Yet more confin'd is pleasure's faithless round:
Fair op'ning to the sight, when first we run,
But ah! how alter'd, when again begun!
When tir'd we view the same known prospect o'er,
And lagging, tread the steps we trod before.
Now clogg'd with spleen, the lazy current flows,
Through doubts, and fears, and self-augmenting woes;
'Till sated, loathing, hopeless here of bliss,
Some plunge to seek it into death's abyss.

   Of all superfluous wealth's unnumber'd stings,
The sharpest is that knowledge which it brings;
Enjoyment purchas'd makes its object known,
And then, alas! each soft illusion's flown:
Love's promis'd sweet, ambition's lofty scheme,
The painter's image, and the poet's theme.

   These, in perspective fair exalted high,
Attract with seeming charms the distant eye;
But when by envious Fortune plac'd too near,
Mis-shapen forms, and grosser tints appear:
Where lovely Venus led her beauteous train,
Some fiend gigantic holds her monstrous reign;
Crowns, scepters, laurels are confus'dly strow'd,
A wild, deform'd, unmeaning, heavy load.

Some pleasures here with sparing hand are giv'n,
That sons of earth should taste their promis'd heaven;
But what was meant to urge us to the chace,
Now stops, or sideway turns our devious race:—
Though still, to make the destin'd course more plain,
Thick are our erring paths beset with pain;
Nor has one object equal charms to prove
The fitting center of our restless love.
And when the great Creator's will had join'd,
Unequal pair! the body and the mind,
Lest the proud spirit should neglect her clay,
He bad corporeal objects thought convey;
Each strong sensation to the soul impart,
Ecstatic transport or afflicting smart:
By that-entic'd, the useful she enjoys;
By this deterr'd, she flies whate'er destroys:
Hence from the dagger's point sharp anguish flows,
And the soft couch is spread with sweet repose.
 In something frail, though gen'ral this design,
For some exceptions every rule confine:
Yet few were they, while nature's genuine store
Supply'd our wants, nor man yet sought for more;
Ere diff'rent mixtures left no form the same,
And vicious habits chang'd our sickly frame.
Now subtle art may gild the venom'd pill,
And bait with soothing sweets destructive ill.
 To narrow self heav'n's impulse unconfin'd,
Diffusive reigns, and takes in all our kind.—

The

The smile of joy reflected joy imparts;
The wretch's groans pierce sympathizing hearts.
Yet not alike are all conjoin'd with all,
Nor throng with rival heat to nature's call:
By varying instinct diffcrent ties are known,
While love superior points to each his own;
Those next the reach of our assisting hands,
And those to whom we're link'd by kindred bands;
Those who most want, and best deserve our care,
In warmer streams the sacred influence share:
Ambrosial sweets her infant's lip distils,
While through the mother's heart quick rapture thrills.
The social fires friend, servant, neighbour claim,
Which blaze collected in the patriot's flame:
Hence Britain throbs superior in thy soul,
Nor idly wak'st thou for the distant pole.

 Yet farther still the saving instinct moves,
And to the future wide extends our loves;
Glows in our bosom for an unborn race,
And warms us mutual to the kind embrace.
For this, to man was giv'n the graceful air;
For this, was woman form'd divinely fair.

 But now to pleasure sensual views confin'd,
Reach not the use, for which it was design'd:
To this one point our hopes, our wishes tend,
And thus mistake the motive for the end.
What'er sensations from enjoyment flow,
Our erring thought to matter's force would owe;

To that afcribe our pleafures and our pains,
And blindly for the caufe miftake the means;
In od'rous meads the vernal gale we praife,
Or dread the ftorm, that blows the wintry feas;
While he's unheeded, who alone can move,
Claims all our fears, and merits all our love;
Alone to fouls can fenfe and thought convey,
Through the dark manfions of furrounding clay.

   Man, part from heav'n, and part from humble earth,
A motley fubftance, takes his various birth;
Clofe link'd to both, he hangs in diff'rent chains,
The pliant fetter length'ning as he ftrains.
If, bravely confcious of her native fires,
To the bold height his nobler frame afpires;
Near as fhe foars to join th' approaching fkies,
Our earth ftill leffens to her diftant eyes.
But if o'erpois'd fhe finks, her downward courfe
Each moment weighs, with ftill augmenting force;
Low and more low, the burthen'd fpirit bends,
While weaker ftill each heav'nly link extends;
'Till proftrate, grov'ling, fetter'd to the ground,
She lies in matter's heap o'erwhelm'd and bound.
Wrapt in the toils of fin, juft heav'n employs
What caus'd her guilt, to blaft her lawlefs joys:
Love, potent guardian of our length'ning race,
Unnerves the feeble lecher's cold embrace;
And appetite, by nature giv'n to fave,
Sinks the gorg'd glutton in his early grave.

What sends yon fleet o'er boist'rous seas to roll,
Beneath the burning line, and frozen pole?
Why ravage men the hills, the plains, the woods?
Why spoil all nature, earth, and air, and floods?
Seek they some prize to help a sinking state?
No!—this must all be done ere * Bernard eat.
Tell it some untaught savage! with surprize
He asks, " How vast must be that giant's size!
" How great his pow'r, who thousands can employ!
" How great his force, who millions can destroy!"
But if the savage would, more curious, know
What potent virtues from such viands flow,
What blest effects they cause——consult with Sloane,†
Let him explain the colic, gout, and stone!

Pleasure's for use; it differs in degree,
Proportion'd to the thing's necessity.
Hence various objects variously excite,
And diff'rent is the date of each delight;
But when th' allotted end we once attain,
Each step beyond it, is a step to pain.
Nor let us murmur.—Hath not earth a store
For every want? it was not meant for more.

Blest is the man, as far as earth can bless,
Whose measur'd passions reach no wild excess;
Who, urg'd by nature's voice, her gifts enjoys,
Nor other means, than nature's force, employs.

* A Frenchman render'd famous for a most extravagant expence in eating.
† Sir Hans Sloane.

While warm with youth the fprightly current flows,
Each vivid fenfe with vig'rous rapture glows;
And when he droops beneath the hand of age,
No vicious habit ftings with fruitlefs rage;
Gradual, his ftrength, and gay fenfations ceafe,
While joys tumultuous fink in filent peace.

 Far other is his lot, who, not content
With what the bounteous care of nature meant,
With labour'd fkill would all her joys dilate,
Sublime their fenfe, and lengthen out their date:
Add, blend, compofe, each various mixture try,
And wind up appetite to luxury.
Thus guilty art unknown defires implants,
And viler arts muft fatisfy their wants;
When to corruption by himfelf betray'd,
Gold blinds the flave, whom luxury has made.

 The hand that form'd us, muft fome ufe intend,
It gives us pow'rs proportion'd to that end;
And happinefs may juftly be defin'd,
A full attainment of the end defign'd.
Virtue and wifdom this alike implies,
And bleft muft be the virtuous and the wife.

 Blifs is ordain'd for all, fince heav'n intends
All beings fhould attain their deftin'd ends:
For this the fair idea fhines confefs'd
To every mind, and glows in every breaft.
Compar'd with this, all mortal joys are vain;
Infpir'd by this, we reftlefs onward ftrain.

             High

High though we mount, the object mounts more high,
Eludes our grasp, and mingles with the sky.
With nothing less th' aspiring soul's content,
For nothing less her gen'rous flame was meant;
Th' unerring rule, which all our steps should guide,
The certain test, by which true good is try'd.
Blest when we reach it, wretched while we miss,
Our joys, our sorrows prove, there must be bliss.
Nor can this be some visionary dream,
Where heated fancy forms the flatt'ring scheme.
There sure is bliss—else, why by all desir'd?
What guileful pow'r has the mad search inspir'd?
Could accident produce in all the same,
Or a vain shadow raise a real flame?
When nature in the world's distended space,
Or fill'd, or almost fill'd each smaller place;
Careful in meanest matter to produce
Each single motion for some certain use;
Hard was the lot of her first fav'rite, man,
Faulty the scheme of his contracted span,
If that alone must know an useless void,
And he feel longings ne'er to be enjoy'd.

 That only can produce consummate joy,
Which equals all the pow'rs it would employ;
Such fitting object to each talent giv'n,
Earth cannot fit what was design'd for heav'n.
Why then is man with gifts sublimest fraught,
And active will, and comprehensive thought?

For

For what is all this waste of mental force?
What! for a house, a coach, a dog, a horse?
Has nature's Lord inverted nature's plan?
Is man now made for what was made for man?
   There must be pleasures past the reach of sense,
Some nobler source must happiness dispense:
Reason, arise! and vindicate thy claim,
Flash on our minds the joy-infusing flame;
Pour forth the fount of light, whose endless store
Thought drinks insatiate, while it thirsts for more.
And thou, seraphic flame! who could'st inspire
The prophet's voice, and wrap his soul in fire;
Ray of th' eternal beam! who canst pervade
The distant past, and future's gloomy shade:
While trembling reason tempts heav'n's dazzling height,
Sublime her force, and guide her dubious flight;
Strengthen'd by thee, she bears the streaming blaze,
And drinks new light from truth's immortal rays.
Great, only evidence of things divine!
By thee reveal'd, the mystic wonders shine!
What puzzled sophists vainly would explore,
What humbled pride in silence must adore,
What plainly mark'd in heav'n's deliver'd page,
Makes the taught hind more wise than Greece's sage.
Yet reason proves thee in her low degree,
And owns thy truths, from their necessity.
  Conspicuous now is happiness display'd,
Possessing him for whom alone we're made,

For he alone all human bliss compleats,
To him alone th' expanding bosom-beats;
Who fills each faculty, each pow'r can move,
Exerts all thought, and deep absorbs all love;
Whose ceaseless being years would tell in vain,
Whose attributes immense all bounds disdain.
No sickly taste the heav'nly rapture cloys,
Nor wearied senses sink in whelming joys;
While, rais'd above low matter's grosser frame,
Pure spirit blazes in his purer flame.
Such are th' immortal blessings that attend
The just and good, the patriot and the friend.
Nor such alone in distant prospect cheer,
They taste heav'n's joys anticipated here.
These in the smiling cups of pleasure flow,
Or, mingling, sooth the bitter stream of woe;
These pay the loss of honours, and of place,
And teach that guilt alone is true disgrace;
These with the glorious exile cheerful rove,
And, far from courts, fresh bloom in Curio's grove.
 Long may such bliss, by such enjoy'd, attest,
The greatly virtuous are the greatly blest!
Enough there are amidst yon gorgeous train,
Who, wretched, prove all other joys are vain.
 So shines the truth these humble lines unfold,
", Fair virtue ever is unwisely sold."
Too mean a price sublimest fortune brings,
Too mean the wealth, the smiles, the crowns of kings:

            For

For rais'd o'er thefe, fhe makes our blifs fecure,
The prefent pleafing, and the future fure:
While profp'rous guilt a sad reverfe appears,
And in the taftelefs now, the future fears.

An EPISTLE to a LADY.

By the Same.

CLarinda, dearly lov'd, attend
The counfels of a faithful friend;
Who with the warmeft wifhes fraught,
Feels all, at leaft, that friendfhip ought.
But fince by ruling heav'n's defign,
Another's fate fhall influence thine;
O! may thefe lines for him prepare
A blifs, which I would die to fhare!

 Man may for wealth or glory roam,
But woman muft be bleft at home;
To this fhould all her ftudies tend,
This her great object and her end.
Diftafte unmingled pleafures bring,
And ufe can blunt affliction's fting;
Hence perfect blifs no mortals know,
And few are plung'd in utter woe;
While nature arm'd againft defpair,
Gives pow'r to mend, or ftrength to bear;

And

And half the thought content may gain,
Which spleen employs to purchase pain.

Trace not the fair domestic plan,
From what you would, but what you can!
Nor, peevish, spurn the scanty store,
Because you think you merit more!
Bliss ever differs in degree,
Thy share alone is meant for thee;
And thou should'st think, however small,
That share enough, for 'tis thy all:
Vain scorn will aggravate distress,
And only make that little less.

Admit whatever trifles come,
Units compose the largest sum:
O! tell them o'er, and say how vain
Are those which form ambition's train:
Which swell the monarch's gorgeous state,
And bribe to ill the guilty Great!
But thou more blest, more wise than these,
Shalt build up happiness on ease.

Hail sweet Content! where joy serene
Gilds the mild soul's unruffled scene;
And with blith fancy's pencil wrought,
Spreads the white web of flowing thought;
Shines lovely in the cheerful face,
And cloaths each charm with native grace;
Effusion pure of bliss sincere,
A vestment for a god to wear.

Far other ornaments compose
The garb that shrouds dissembled woes,
Piec'd out with motley dies and sorts,
Freaks, whimsies, festivals, and sports;
The troubled mind's fantastic dress,
Which madness titles happiness.
While the gay wretch to revel bears
The pale remains of sighs and tears:
And seeks in crowds, like her undone,
What only can be found in one.

But, chief, my gentle friend! remove
Far from thy couch seducing love!
O! shun the false magician's art,
Nor trust thy yet unguarded heart!
Charm'd by his spells fair honour flies,
And thousand treach'rous phantoms rise,
Where guilt in beauty's ray beguiles,
And ruin lurks in friendship's smiles.
Lo! where th' enchanted captive dreams
Of warbling groves and purling streams;
Of painted meads, of flowers that shed
Their odours round her fragrant bed.
Quick shifts the scene, the charm is lost,
She wakes upon a desert coast!
No friendly hand to lend its aid,
No guardian bow'r to spread its shade;
Expos'd to every chilling blast,
She treads th' inhospitable waste;

And down the drear decline of life,
Sinks a forlorn, dishonour'd wife.

 Neglect not thou the voice of Fame,
But clear from crime, be free from blame!
Though all were innocence within,
'Tis guilt to wear the garb of sin.
Virtue rejects the foul disguise:
None merit praise who praise despise.

 Slight not, in supercilious strain,
Long practis'd modes, as low or vain!
The world will vindicate their cause,
And claim blind faith in custom's laws.
Safer with multitudes to stray,
Than tread alone a fairer way;
To mingle with the erring throng,
Than boldly speak ten millions wrong.

 Beware of the relentless train,
Who forms adore, whom forms maintain!
Lest prudes demure, or coxcombs loud,
Accuse thee to the partial crowd;
Foes who the laws of honour slight,
A judge who measures guilt by spite.

 Behold the sage Aurelia stand,
Disgrace and fame at her command!
As if heaven's delegate design'd,
Sole arbiter of all her kind.
Whether she try some favour'd piece,
By rules devis'd in ancient Greece;

Or whether modern in her flight,
She tells what Paris thinks polite.
For much her talents to advance,
She study'd Greece, and travell'd France.
There learn'd the happy art to please,
With all the charms of labour'd ease;
Through looks and nods with meaning fraught,
To teach what she was never taught.

 By her each latent spring is seen,
The workings foul of secret spleen;
The guilt that sculks in fair pretence,
Or folly veil'd in specious sense.
And much her righteous spirit grieves,
When worthlessness the world deceives;
Whether the erring crowd commends
Some patriot sway'd by private ends;
Or husband trust a faithless wife,
Secure in ignorance from strife.
Averse she brings their deeds to view,
But justice claims the rig'rous due;
Humanely anxious to produce
At least some possible excuse.
O ne'er may virtue's dire disgrace
Prepare a triumph for the base!

 Mere forms the fool implicit sway,
Which witlings with contempt survey,
Blind folly no defect can see,
Half wisdom views but one degree;

The

The wife remoter ufes reach,
Which judgment and experience teach.
   Whoever would be pleas'd, and pleafe,
Muft do what others do with eafe.
Great precept undefin'd by rule,
And only learn'd in cuftom's fchool;
To no peculiar form confin'd,
It fpreads through all the human kind;
Beauty and wit and worth fupplies,
Yet graceful in the good and wife.
Rich with this gift and none befide,
In fafhion's ftream how many glide?
Secure from every mental woe,
From treach'rous friend or open foe;
From focial fympathy that fhares
The public lofs or private cares;
Whether the barb'rous foe invade,
Or merit pine in fortune's fhade.
   Hence gentle Anna ever gay,
The fame to-morrow as to-day.
Save where perchance, when others weep,
Her cheek the decent forrow fteep;
Save when perhaps a melting tale,
O'er every tender breaft prevail.
The good, the bad, the great, the fmall,
She likes, fhe loves, fhe honours all.
And yet if fland'rous malice blame,
Patient fhe yields a fifter's fame.

Alike

Alike if satire or if praise,
She says whate'er the circle says;
Implicit does whate'er we do,
Without one point or wish in view,
Sure test of others, faithful glass
Through which the various phantoms pass,
Wide blank, unfeeling when alone,
No care, no joy, no thought her own.

 Not thus succeeds the peerless dame,
Who looks, and talks, and acts for fame;
Intent, so wide her cares extend,
To make the universe her friend.
Now with the gay in frolic shines,
Now reasons deep with deep divines.
With courtiers now extols the great,
With patriots sighs o'er Britain's fate.
Now breathes with zealots holy fires,
Now melts in less refin'd desires.
Doom'd to exceed in each degree,
Too wise, too week, too proud, too free,
Too various for one single word,
The high sublime of deep absurd.
While every talent nature grants,
Just serves to shew how much she wants.

 Although in ——— combine
The virtues of our sex and thine:
Her hand restrains the widow's tears,
Her sense informs, and sooths and cheers;

Yet

Yet like an angel in disguise,
She shines but to some favour'd eyes;
Nor is the distant herd allow'd
To view the radiance through the cloud.
　But thine is every winning art,
Thine is the friendly honest heart:
And should the gen'rous spirit flow,
Beyond where prudence fears to go;
Such sallies are of nobler kind,
Than virtues of a narrow mind.

An EPISTLE to Mr. POPE.

By the Same.

HEAVEN in the human breast implants
　Fit appetites for all our wants;
With hunger prompts to strength'ning food,
With love of praise to public good;
These to their object strait convey,
While reason winds her tardy way.
　Yet in one center should unite,
Faith, instinct, reason, appetite:
One perfect plan ordain'd to trace,
And nature dignify with grace;
In one great system meant to roll,
To move, support, and guide the whole.

But some there are who rigid blame
The mind that thirsts for righteous fame;
And with weak lights presumptuous scan
The springs which move predestin'd man.
And some there are, (accurs'd their art!)
Though all the nine their charms impart,
Who in false forms of great and just,
Cloath av'rice, treachery, rage and lust:
As if superior beings suit
Those attributes which sink the brute.
But vainly chime the partial lays,
Chaste Fame rejects all spurious praise.
She, fairest offspring of the skies,
The goddess of the brave and wise,
Whose sacred impulse prompts the best
To succour and preserve the rest,
Is deaf to every private call,
And wakes but at the voice of all.

From heaps of ill-collected gain,
From hecatombs by heroes slain,
From courts, where guilty greatness dwells,
She flies to penury and cells;
With Erskine, pious exile, goes,
To sooth a drooping father's woes;
Or mingling with the orphan-train,
She sings the bounties of Germain *.

* Lady Elizabeth Germain.

Nor

Nor pow'r, nor policy of state,
Can ever give intrinsic weight:
And should fallacious art display
O'er titled dross a golden ray,
Still baser through detecting years,
The speckled counterfeit appears.

But when from proof, fair issuing forth,
The ore asserts its native worth;
Then, sov'reign bard, 'tis justly thine
To stamp the well-attested coin;
And consecrated with thy name,
To treasure in the stores of Fame.

EPISTLE to POLLIO, from the Hills of HOWTH in IRELAND.

By the Same.

POLLIO! would'st thou condescend
 Here to see thy humble friend,
Far from doctors, potions, pills,
Drinking health on native hills;

Thou the precious draught may'st share,
Lucy shall the bowl prepare.
From the brousing goat it flows,
From each balmy shrub that grows;
Hence the kidling's wanton fire,
Hence the nerves that brace his sire.
Vigorous, buxom, young and gay,
Thou like them shalt love and play.

 What, though far from silver Thames,
Stately piles, and courtly dames;
Here we boast a purer flood,
Joys that stream from sprightly blood;
Here is simple beauty seen,
Fair, and cloath'd like beauty's queen:
Nature's hands the garbs compose,
From the lilly and the rose.
Or, if charm'd with richer dies,
Fancy every robe supplies.
Should perchance some high-born fair,
Absent, claim thy tender care;
Here, enraptur'd shalt thou trace,
S——'s shape, and R——'s face;
While the waking dream shall pay
Many a wishing, hopeless day.
Domes with gold and toil unbought,
Rise by magic pow'r of thought,
Where by artist's hand undrawn,
Slopes the vale, and spreads the lawn;

As if sportive nature meant,
Here to mock the works of Kent [a].
　Come, and with thee bring along
Jocund tale and witty song,
Sense to teach, and words to move,
Arts that please, adorn, improve;
And, to gild the glorious scene,
Conscience spotless and serene.
　Poor with all a HEATHCOTE's [b] store,
Lives the man who pines for more.
Wretched he who doom'd to roam,
Never can be blest at home;
Nor retire within his mind,
From th' ungrateful and unkind.
Happy they whom crowds befriend,
Curs'd who on the crowd depend;
On the great one's peevish fit,
On the coxcomb's spurious wit;

---

[a] William Kent, a painter, an architect, and the father of modern gardening. "In the first character," says Mr. Walpole, "he was below "mediocrity; in the second, he was a restorer of the science; in the "last, an original, and the inventor of an art that realizes painting "and improves nature. Mahomet imagined an Elysium, but Kent "created many." See Anecdotes of Painting, vol. v. p. 111. Mr. Kent died April 12, 1748.

[b] Sir Gilbert Heathcote, Knt. and Bart. Alderman of London, and Father of the City. He was reputed the richest Commoner in Great Britain at the time of his death, 25th of January 1733.

Ever sentenc'd to bemoan
Others failings in their own.
  If, like them, rejecting ease,
Hills and health no longer please;
Quick descend!—— Thou may'st resort
To the viceroy's splendid court.
There, indignant, shalt thou see
Cringing slaves, who might be free,
Brib'd with titles, hope, or gain,
Tye their country's shameful chain;
Or, inspir'd by heav'n's good cause,
Waste the land with holy laws:
While the gleanings of their power,
Lawyers, lordlings, priests devour.
  Now, methinks, I hear thee say,
" Drink alone thy mountain-whey!
" Wherefore tempt the Irish shoals?
" Sights like these are nearer Paul's."

An ODE to WILLIAM PULTNEY, Esq;

By the Same.

I.

REMOTE from liberty and truth [a],
  By fortune's crime, my early youth
    Drank error's poison'd springs.
Taught by dark creeds and mystic law,
Wrapt up in reverential awe,
    I bow'd to priests and kings.

II.

Soon reason dawn'd, with troubled sight
I caught the glimpse of painful light,
    Afflicted and afraid,
Too weak it shone to mark my way,
Enough to tempt my steps to stray
    Along the dubious shade.

III.

Restless I roam'd, when from afar
Lo, HOOKER shines! the friendly star

---

[a] Alluding to the Author's having been educated in the Roman Catholic religion.

Sends

Sends forth a steady ray.
Thus cheer'd, and eager to pursue,
I mount 'till glorious to my view,
   Locke spreads the realms of day.

IV.

Now warm'd with noble Sidney's page,
I pant with all the patriot's rage;
   Now wrapt in Plato's dream,
With More and Harrington around
I tread fair Freedom's magic ground,
   And trace the flatt'ring scheme.

V.

But soon the beauteous vision flies;
And hideous spectres now arise,
   Corruption's direful train:
The partial judge perverting laws,
The priest forsaking virtue's cause,
   And senates slaves to gain.

VI.

Vainly the pious artist's toil
Would rear to heaven a mortal pile,
   On some immortal plan;
Within a sure, though varying date,
Confin'd, alas! is every state
   Of empire and of man.

VII.

What though the good, the brave, the wise,
With adverse force undaunted rise,

To break th' eternal doom!
Though CATO liv'd, though TULLY spoke,
Though BRUTUS dealt the godlike stroke,
  Yet perish'd fated ROME.

VIII.

To swell some future tyrant's pride,
Good FLEURY [b] pours the golden tide
  On Gallia's smiling shores;
Once more her fields shall thirst in vain
For wholsome streams of honest gain,
  While rapine wastes her stores.

IX.

Yet glorious is the great design,
And such, O PULTNEY! such is thine,
  To prop a nation's frame.
If crush'd beneath the sacred weight,
The ruins of a falling state
  Shall tell the patriot's name.

---

[b] Cardinal Fleury, Preceptor to Lewis XVth, and afterwards Prime Minister of France.

An ODE to the Right Honourable the Lord LONSDALE[a].

By the Same.

I.

LONSDALE! thou ever honour'd name,
 For such is sacred virtue's claim,
  Say, why! my noble friend!
While nature sheds her balmy powers
 O'er hill and dale, in leaves and flowers,
  Say, why my joys suspend!

II.

Here spreads the lawn high-crown'd with wood,
Here slopes the vale, there winds the flood
  In many a crystal maze.
The fishes sport, in silver pride
Slow moves the swan, on either side
  The herds promiscuous graze.

III.

Or if the stiller shade you love,
Here solemn nods th' imbow'ring grove

---

[a] Henry Lowther, Lord Viscount Lonsdale. He died 6th of March 1751.

O'er innocence and ease;
Whether with deep reflection fraught,
Or in the sprightly stream of thought,
   The lighter trifles please.

IV.

[b] And should the shaft of treacherous spleen
Glance venom'd through this peaceful scene,
   Unheeded may it fly!
Provok'd, nor tempted to repay,
Though truth severer prompt the lay,
   A mean prosaic lie.

V.

Here with the pheasant and the hare,
Unfearful of the human snare,
   Have statesmen pass'd a day:
While far from yon forbidden gate,
Pale care and lank remorse await
   Their slow-returning prey.

VI.

O! blind to all the joys of life,
Who seek them in the storm of strife,
   Destroying, or destroy'd.
Less wretched they, and yet unbless'd,
Who batten in lethargic rest,
   On blessings unenjoy'd.

VII.

But come, my friend, the sun invites,
For thee the town hath no delights,

[b] Alluding to a certain scandalous libel.

Distasted

Diſtaſted and aggriev'd;
While fools believe, while villains cheat,
'Too honeſt to approve deceit,
   Too wiſe to be deceiv'd.

VIII.

Or doſt thou fear leſt dire diſeaſe
Again thy tortur'd frame may ſeize;
   And haſt thou therefore ſtay'd?
O! rather haſte, where thou ſhalt find
A ready hand, a gentle mind,
   To comfort and to aid.

IX.

And while by ſore afflictions try'd,
You bear without the Stoic's pride,
   What Stoic never bore;
O! may I learn like thee to bear,
And what ſhall be my deſtin'd ſhare,
   To ſuffer, not explore.

An ODE.

By the Same.

GENTLE, idle, trifling boy,
   Sing of pleaſures, ſing of joy!
Well you paint the cryſtal ſpring,
Well the flow'ry meadow ſing.

                                        But

But beware with bolder flight,
Tempt not heaven's unequal height;
But beware! with impious strain,
Mock not freedom's hallow'd train!
Sacred, here, O! ever be
Heaven, and heaven-born liberty!
   Let the slaves of lawless sway,
Let the stupid flock obey!
Pent within a narrow fold,
Ty'd, and stript, and slain, and sold.
Happier stars the brave befriend,
Britons know a nobler end.
Theirs it is to temper laws;
Theirs to watch in freedom's cause,
Theirs one common good to share,
Theirs to feel one common care;
In the glorious task combin'd,
From the monarch to the hind.
   Yet O! cease not, gentle boy!
Sing of pleasures, sing of joy!
Like thy brothers of the wing,
Idly hop, and chirp, and sing.
Heaven can nothing vain produce,
Ev'ry creature has its use.
Thine it is to sooth our toil,
Thine to make e'en wisdom smile.
Much they err who such despise,
Trifles please the truly wise.

An ODE.

By the Same.

I.

ON Stow, the Muse's happy theme,
   Let fancy's eye enamour'd gaze;
Where through one nobly simple scheme,
   Ten thousand varying beauties please.
There patriot-virtue rears her shrine,
Nor, love! art thou depriv'd of thine.

II.

Mark where from POPE's exhaustless vein,
   Pure flows the stream of copious thought,
While nature pours the genial strain,
   With fairest springs of learning fraught;
The treasures of each clime and age,
Grace and enrich his sacred page.

III.

So while through Britain's fields her Thames
   Prolific rolls his silver tide;
The tribute of a thousand streams
   Swells the majestic river's pride;
And where his gen'rous current strays,
The wealth of either world conveys.

IV.

Far other is that wretch's song,
    Whose scanty rill devoid of force,
With idle tinklings creeps along,
    A narrow, crooked, dubious course:
Or foul with congregated floods,
Spreads a wide waste o'er plains and woods.

V.

In action thus the mind express'd
    High soars in Pope the true sublime:
A Stow unfolds a Cobham's breast,
    A Bavius crawls in doggrel rhyme.
Through all their various works we trace
The greatly virtuous, and the base.

An ODE.

By the Same.

I.

TOO anxious for the public weal,
    Awhile suspend the toilsome strife!
O think if Britain claims thy zeal,
    Thy friends and Britain claim thy life!

II.

Thy gen'rous, free, and active foul,
    Infpir'd by glory's facred flame,
Springs ardent to the diftant goal,
    And ftrains the weaker mortal frame.

III.

Happy whom reafon deigns to guide,
    Secure within the golden mean,
Who fhuns the Stoic's fenfelefs pride,
    Nor wallows with the herd obfcene.

IV.

He nor with brow feverely bent,
    Chides pleafure's fmiling train away;
Nor carelefs of life's great intent,
    With folly waftes each heedlefs day.

V.

But from the mountain's lofty height,
    Now nature's mighty frame furveys:
And now defcending with delight,
    Along the humble valley ftrays.

VI.

So have I feen thee gain applaufe,
    Though faction rag'd, from Britain's peers;
Then glorious in thy country's caufe,
    Go whifper love in Chloe's ears.

An ODE to MANKIND.

Address'd to the PRINCE[a].

By the Same.

INTRODUCTION to the PRINCE.

NOR me the glories of thy birth engage,
    With royal names to swell my pompous page:
Nor meaner views allure, in soothing lays
To court thy favour with officious praise.
Yet praise it is, thus to address thine ear
In strains no slave dare sing, no tyrant hear;
While warm for Britain's rights and nature's laws,
I call forth Britain's HOPE in freedom's cause:
Assert an empire which to ALL belongs,
And vindicate a world's long-suffer'd wrongs.
    These saving truths import thee most to know,
The links that tie the mighty to the low;
What now, our fellow-subject, is your due,
And, when our lord, shall be a debt on you.
O! may'st thou to the throne such maxims bring!
And feel the free-man while thou reign'st the king.

[a] Frederick Prince of Wales.

Far hence the tribe, whose servile arts delude,
And teach the great to spurn the multitude.
Are those unworthy of the royal heir,
Who claim the future monarch's duteous care?
Still may thy thoughts the godlike task pursue,
And to the many ne'er prefer the few!
Still may'st thou fly thy fortune's specious friends,
Who deal forth sov'reign grace to private ends;
In narrow streams divert the copious tide,
Exalt one sect and damn the world beside:
While with false lights directing partial rule,
The lord of nations falls a party's tool.
Such there have been—and such, in truth's despite,
Disgrac'd the cause of liberty and right.
But thou shalt rise superior to their arts,
And fix thy empire in a people's hearts.

Nor hence may faction boast her favour'd claim,
Where selfish passions borrow virtue's name:
Free government alone preserves the free,
And righteous rule is gen'ral liberty;
Their guiding law is freedom's native voice,
The public good defin'd by public choice;
And justly should the bold offenders fall,
Who dare invade the sov'reign rights of all;
A king who proudly makes these claims his own,
Or they whose rage would shake a lawful throne.
From truths like these proceeds a right divine,
And may the pow'r that rais'd, preserve thy scepter'd line!

To MANKIND: An ODE.

I.

IS there, or do the schoolmen dream?
Is there on earth a pow'r supreme,
  The delegate of heav'n,
To whom an uncontroul'd command,
In every realm o'er sea and land,
  By special grace is giv'n?

II.

Then say, what signs this god proclaim?
Dwells he amidst the diamond's flame,
  A throne his hallow'd shrine?
The borrow'd pomp, the arm'd array,
Want, fear, and impotence betray:
  Strange proofs of pow'r divine!

III.

If service due from human kind,
To men in slothful ease reclin'd,
  Can form a sov'reign's claim:
Hail monarchs! ye, whom heav'n ordains,
Our toils unshar'd, to share our gains,
  Ye ideots, blind and lame!

IV.

Superior virtue, wisdom, might,
Create and mark the ruler's right,
  So reason must conclude:
Then thine it is, to whom belong
The wise, the virtuous, and the strong,
  Thrice sacred multitude!

V.

In thee, vast ALL! are these contain'd,
For thee are those, thy parts ordain'd,
  So nature's systems roll:
The scepter's thine, if such there be;
If none there is, then thou art free,
  Great monarch! mighty whole!

VI.

Let the proud tyrant rest his cause
On faith, prescription, force, or laws,
  An host's or senate's voice!
His voice affirms thy stronger due,
Who for the many made the few,
  And gave the species choice.

VII.

Unsanctify'd by thy command,
Unown'd by thee, the scepter'd hand
  The trembling slave may bind.
But loose from nature's moral ties,
The oath by force impos'd belies
  The unassenting mind.

VIII. Thy

VIII.

Thy will's thy rule, thy good its end;
You punish only to defend
   What parent nature gave:
And he who dares her gifts invade,
By nature's oldest law is made
   Thy victim or thy slave.

IX.

Thus reason founds the just decree
On universal liberty,
   Not private rights resign'd:
Through various nature's wide extent,
No private beings e'er were meant
   To hurt the gen'ral kind.

X.

Thee justice guides, thee right maintains,
Th' oppressor's wrongs, the pilf'rer's gains,
   Thy injur'd weal impair.
Thy warmest passions soon subside,
Nor partial envy, hate, nor pride,
   Thy temper'd counsels share.

XI.

Each instance of thy vengeful rage,
Collected from each clime and age,
   Though malice swell the sum,
Would seem a spotless scanty scroll,
Compar'd with Marius' bloody roll,
   Or Sylla's hippodrome.

XII.

But thine has been imputed blame,
Th' unworthy few aſſume thy name,
   The rabble weak and loud ;
Or thoſe who on thy ruins feaſt,
The lord, the lawyer, and the prieſt ;
   A more ignoble crowd.

XIII.

Avails it thee, if one devours,
Or leſſer ſpoilers ſhare his pow'rs,
   While both thy claim oppoſe ?
Monſters who wore thy ſully'd crown,
Tyrants who pull'd thoſe monſters down,
   Alike to thee were foes.

XIV.

Far other ſhone fair Freedom's hand,
Far other was th' immortal ſtand,
   When Hampden fought for thee :
They ſnatch'd from rapine's gripe thy ſpoils,
The fruits and prize of glorious toils,
   Of arts and induſtry.

XV.

On thee yet foams the preacher's rage,
On thee fierce frowns th' hiſtorian's page,
   A falſe apoſtate train :
Tears ſtream adown the martyr's tomb ;
Unpity'd in their harder doom,
   Thy thouſands ſtrow the plain.

XVI.

These had no charms to please the sense,
No graceful port, no eloquence,
   To win the Muse's throng:
Unknown, unsung, unmark'd they lie;
But Cæsar's fate o'ercasts the sky,
   And Nature mourns his wrong.

XVII.

Thy foes, a frontless band, invade;
Thy friends afford a timid aid,
   And yield up half the right.
Ev'n Locke beams forth a mingled ray,
Afraid to pour the flood of day
   On man's too feeble sight.

XVIII.

Hence are the motley systems fram'd,
Of right transfer'd, of power reclaim'd;
   Distinctions weak and vain.
Wise nature mocks the wrangling herd;
For unreclaim'd, and untransfer'd,
   Her pow'rs and rights remain.

XIX.

While law the royal agent moves,
The instrument thy choice approves,
   We bow through him to you.
But change, or cease th' inspiring choice,
The sov'reign sinks a private voice,
   Alike in one, or few!

XX.

Shall then the wretch, whose dastard heart
Shrinks at a tyrant's nobler part,
   And only dares betray;
With reptile wiles, alas! prevail,
Where force, and rage, and priest-craft fail,
   To pilfer pow'r away?

XXI.

O! shall the bought, and buying tribe,
The slaves who take, and deal the bribe,
   A people's claims enjoy!
So Indian murd'rers hope to gain
The pow'rs and virtues of the slain,
   Of wretches they destroy.

XXII.

" Avert it, heav'n! you love the brave,
" You hate the treach'rous, willing slave,
   " The self-devoted head.
" Nor shall an hireling's voice convey
" That sacred prize to lawless sway,
   " For which a nation bled."

XXIII.

Vain pray'r, the coward's weak resource!
Directing reason, active force,
   Propitious heaven bestows.
But ne'er shall flame the thund'ring sky,
To aid the trembling herd that fly
   Before their weaker foes.

XXIV. In

XXIV.

In names there dwell no magic charms,
The British virtues, British arms
   Unloos'd our fathers' band :
Say, Greece and Rome ! if these should fail,
What names, what ancestors avail,
   To save a sinking land ?

XXV.

Far, far from us such ills shall be,
Mankind shall boast one nation free,
   One monarch truly great :
Whose title speaks a people's choice,
Whose sovereign will a people's voice,
   Whose strength a prosp'rous state.

VERSES to CAMILLA.

By the Same.

WEARY'D with indolent repose,
   A life unmix'd with joys or woes ;
Where all the lazy moments crept,
And every passion sluggish slept ;
I wish'd for love's inspiring pains,
To rouze the loiterer in my veins.
Th' officious power my call attends,
He who uncall'd his succour lends ;

                                  And

And with a smile of wanton spite,
He gave Camilla to my sight.
Her eyes their willing captive seize,
Her look, her air, her manner please;
New beauties please, unseen before,
Or seen, in her they please me more;
And soon, too soon, alas! I find
The virtues of a nobler kind.

Now cheerful springs the morning ray,
Now cheerful sinks the closing day;
For every morn with her I walk'd,
And every eve with her I talk'd;
With her I lik'd the vernal bloom,
With her I lik'd the crowded room;
From her at night I went with pain,
And long'd for morn to meet again.

How quick the smiling moments pass,
Through varying fancy's mimic glass!
While the gay scene is painted o'er,
Where all was one wide blank before;
And sweetly sooth'd th' inchanting dream,
'Till love inspir'd a bolder scheme.

Camilla, stung with grief and shame;
Now marks, and shuns the guilty flame;
Fierce anger lighten'd in her face,
Then cold reserve assum'd its place:
And soon, the wretch's hardest fate,
Contempt succeeds declining hate.

No more my presence now she flies,
She sees me with unheeding eyes;
Sees me with various passions burn,
Enrag'd depart, submiss return;
Return with flattering hopes to find
Soft pity move her gentle mind.
But ah! her looks were still the same,
Unmark'd I went, unmark'd I came;
Unmark'd were all my hopes and fears,
While Strephon whispers in her ears.

O Jealousy! distracting guest!
Fly to some happy lover's breast;
Fitly with joy thou mingleft care,
But why inhabit with despair?

To CLARISSA.

By the Same.

'TWAS when the friendly shade of night
    Suspends the busy cares of light,
And on the various world bestows
Or sprightly joy, or calm repose.
With gen'rous wine the glass was crown'd,
And mirth, and talk, and toasts went round.
   Clarissa came to bless the feast,
Clarissa, dearly welcome guest.

Not such she look'd as when by day
She blazes in the diamond's ray;
And adding to each gem a grace,
Gives India's wealth the second place.
But soft reclin'd in careless ease,
More pleasing, less intent to please.
Loose flow'd her hair in wanton pride,
Her robe unbound, her zone unty'd;
Half bare to view her milk-white breast,
A slender veil scarce shades the rest:
Her eye with sparkling lustre glows,
And wit in sweetest accent flows.

 Now sooth'd the angel's voice I hear,
And drink in love at either ear;
Now stung with wilder rapture gaze,
While our eyes meet with blended rays;
And kindling in th' infectious flame,
I feel what words want pow'r to name.

 Awaking from the silent trance,
Cautious I steal a broken glance;
In clam'rous mirth each pang disguise,
And laughter swell with bursting sighs;
For Envy, pallid fiend, was there,
And Jealousy with watchful care.

 Now ends the feast, each guest retires,
And with them all my soul desires,
Clarissa goes.—Ah! cruel fate!
She goes with her ill-sorted mate.

Sullen and flow he moves along,
And heavy hums a drowfy fong.
O! drowfy may the monfter lye,
And inftant flumbers feal his eye!
So shalt thou, beft belov'd, efcape
The horrors of a legal rape.

  Or, fhould the brutifh inftinct goad,
And thou muft bear th' unwelcome load;
If ftruggle, pray'r, pretence be vain,
To fhun what tyrant-laws ordain;
Ah! fparing deal out fcanty dues,
And keep whate'er thou canft refufe!
Ah! give no bounding pulfe to beat,
No cheek to glow with genial heat!
No breaft to heave in am'rous play,
No limbs to twine, no hands to ftray;
But fluggifh prefs the joylefs bed,
And lie in cold indiff'rence dead:
Nor let the blafting fpoiler fip
The fragrance of thy balmy lip!
To fhare with him the lover's part,
Were rank adultery of the heart.

  But if, in chafter love's defpite,
Warm nature catch the known delight;
While fierce defires tumultuous rife,
And rapture melts thy clofing eyes;
Ah! be thofe joys for me defign'd,
And let me rufh upon thy mind!

To me the burning kiss impart,
On me impress the humid dart,
For me unlock the nectar'd store,
Then sigh, and dream the transport o'er!

 Thus with her lov'd idea fraught,
Delusive fancy charms my thought;
And joining in the flatt'ring cheat,
Willing I hug the dear deceit;
From fiction real bliss receive,
And all I fondly wish believe;
Nor envy to a husband's arms,
The dull fruition of her charms.

 But when, regardless of my truth,
She smiles on some more favour'd youth;
And while he whispers in her ears,
With more than wonted pleasure hears;
My jealous thought his voice supplies,
And reads perdition in her eyes.
Then torn with envy, love, and hate,
I wish her with her wedded mate.

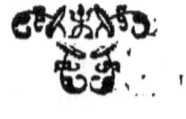

An INSCRIPTION on the TOMB,

Raised to the memory of the Author's father, and of others his ancestors.

By the Same.

UNmark'd by trophies of the great and vain,
   Here sleeps in silent tombs a gentle train.
No folly wasted their paternal store,
No guilt, no sordid av'rice made it more;
With honest fame, and sober plenty crown'd,
They liv'd, and spread their cheering influence round.
May he whose hand this pious tribute pays,
Receive a like return of filial praise!

EPIGRAMS.

By the Same.

EPIGRAM I.

I Lov'd thee beautiful and kind,
   And plighted an eternal vow
So alter'd are thy face and mind
'Twere perjury to love thee now.

EPIGRAM II.

SINCE first you knew my am'rous smart,
    Each day augments your proud disdain;
'Twas then enough to break my heart,
And now, thank heav'n! to break my chain.
Cease, thou scorner, cease to shun me!
Now let love and hatred cease!
Half that rigour had undone me,
All that rigour gives me peace.

EPIGRAM III.

MY heart still hovering round about you,
    I thought I could not live without you;
Now we have liv'd three months asunder,
How I liv'd with you is the wonder.

EPIGRAM IV.

Upon the Bust of English Worthies, at Stow.

AMONG these chiefs of British race,
    Who live in breathing stone,
Why has not COBHAM's bust a place?
    The structure was his own.

EPIGRAM V.

THO' cheerful, discreet, and with freedom well bred,
    She never repented an idle word said:
Securely she smiles on the forward and bold,
They feel what they owe her, and feel it untold.

EPIGRAM VI.

LYE on! while my revenge shall be,
  To speak the very truth of thee.

EPIGRAM VII.

I Swore I lov'd, and you believ'd,
  Yet, trust me, we were both deceiv'd;
Though all I swore was true.
I lov'd one gen'rous, good, and kind,
A form created in my mind;
  And thought that form was you.

EPIGRAM VIII.

On Mrs. PENELOPE.

THE gentle Pen, with look demure,
  Awhile was thought a virgin pure;
But Pen, as ancient poets say,
Undid by night the work of day.

EPIGRAM IX.

On one who first abused, and then made love to a LADY.

FOUL —— with graceless verse,
  The noble —— dar'd asperse.
But when he saw her well bespatter'd,
Her reputation stain'd and tatter'd;

He gaz'd and lov'd the hideous elf,
She look'd so very like himself.
True sung the bard well known to fame *,
Self-love and social are the same.

EPIGRAM X.

WHILE Lucy, chaste as mountain snows,
   Gives every idle fop a hearing;
In Mary's breast a passion glows,
   Which stronger is from not appearing.
Say, who has chose the better part?
   Mary, to whom no joy is missing;
Or she, who, dupe to her own heart,
   Pays the full price of Mary's kissing.

EPIGRAM XI.

SHE who in secret yields her heart,
   Again may claim it from her lover;
But she who plays the trifler's part,
   Can ne'er her squander'd fame recover.
Then grant the boon for which I pray!
'Tis better lend than throw away.

EPIGRAM XII.

WE thought you without titles great,
   And wealthy with a small estate;
While by your humble self alone,
You seem'd unrated and unknown.

* Mr. Pope.

But now on fortune's swelling tide
High-borne, in all the pomp of pride;
Of grandeur vain, and fond of pelf,
'Tis plain, my lord, you knew yourself.

EPIGRAM XIII.

Lovely shines thy wedded fair,
 Gentle as the yielding air;
Cheering as the solar beam,
Soothing as the fountain stream.
 Why then, jealous husband, rail?
All may breathe the ambient gale,
Bask in heaven's diffusive ray,
Drink the streams that pass away.
All may share unless'ning joy,
Why then jealous, peevish boy?
Water, air, and light confine,
Ere thou think'st her only thine.

EPIGRAM XIV.

Tom thought a wild profusion great,
 And therefore spent his whole estate:
Will thinks the wealthy are ador'd,
And gleans what misers blush to hoard.
Their passion, merit, fate the same,
They thirst and starve alike for fame.

EPIGRAM XV.

To Clarissa.

WHY like a tyrant wilt thou reign,
    When thou may'ſt rule the willing mind?
Can the poor pride of giving pain
Repay the joys that wait the kind?
I curſe my fond enduring heart,
Which ſcorn'd preſumes not to be free,
Condemn'd to feel a double ſmart,
To hate myſelf, and burn for thee.

EPIGRAM XVI.

EVER buſy'd, ne'er employ'd,
    Ever loving, ne'er enjoy'd,
Ever doom'd to ſeek and miſs,
And pay unbleſs'd the price of bliſs.

EPIGRAM XVII.

VAINLY hath heaven denounc'd the woman's woes,
    Thou know'ſt no tender cares, no bitter throes,
Unfelt your offspring comes, unfelt it goes.

The Danger of Writing Verse.

An Epistle.

First printed in the Year 1741.

By WILLIAM WHITEHEAD, Esq;

Quæ poterant unquam satis expurgare cicutæ,
Ni melius dormire putem, quam scribere versus?
Hor. Ep 2. Lib. 2.

YOU ask me, sir, why thus by phantoms aw'd,
   No kind occasion tempts the Muse abroad?
Why, when retirement sooths this idle art,
To fame regardless sleeps the youthful heart?
   'Twould wrong your judgment, should I fairly say
Distrust or weakness caus'd the cold delay:
Hint the small diff'rence, till we touch the lyre,
'Twixt real genius and too strong desire;
The human slips, or seeming slips pretend,
That rouze the critic, but escape the friend;
Nay which, though dreadful when the foe pursues,
You pass, and smile, and still provoke the Muse.
   Yet, spite of all you think, or kindly feign,
My hand will tremble while it grasps the pen.
For not in this, like other arts, we try
Our light excursions in a summer sky,

No casual flights the dangerous trade admits,
But wits once authors, are for ever wits.
The fool in prose, like earth's unwieldy son,
May oft rise vig'rous, though he's oft o'erthrown;
One dangerous crisis marks our rise or fall,
By all we're courted, or we're shun'd by all.

   Will it avail, that unmatur'd by years,
My easy numbers pleas'd your partial ears,
If now condemn'd, my riper lays must bear
The wise man's censure, and the vain man's sneer?
Or, still more hard, ev'n where he's valu'd most,
The man must suffer, if the poet's lost;
For wanting wit, be totally undone,
And barr'd all arts, for having fail'd in one.
When fears like these his serious thoughts engage,
No bugbear phantom curbs the poet's rage;
'Tis powerful reason holds the streighten'd rein,
While flutt'ring fancy to the distant plain
Sends a long look, and spreads her wings in vain.

   But grant, for once, th' officious Muse has shed
Her gentlest influence on his infant head,
Let fears lie vanquish'd, and resounding Fame
Give to the bellowing blast the poet's name.
And see! distinguish'd from the crowd he moves,
Each finger marks him, and each eye approves!
Secure, as halcyons brooding o'er the deep,
The waves roll gently, and the thunders sleep,

Obsequious

Obsequious nature binds the tempest's wings,
And pleas'd attention listens whilst he sings!
   O blissful state, O more than human joy!
What shafts can reach him, or what cares annoy?
What cares, my friend? why all that man can know,
Oppress'd with real or with fancy'd woe.
Rude to the world, like earth's first lord expell'd,
To climes unknown, from Eden's safer field;
No more eternal springs around him breathe,
Black air scowls o'er him, deadly damps beneath;
Now must he learn, misguided youth, to bear
Each varying season of the poet's year:
Flatt'ry's full beam, detraction's wintry store,
The frowns of fortune, or the pride of pow'r.
His acts, his words, his thoughts no more his own,
Each folly blazon'd, and each frailty known.
Is he reserv'd?—his sense is so refin'd,
It ne'er descends to trifle with mankind:
Open and free?—they find the secret cause
Is vanity; He courts the world's applause.
Nay, though he speak not, something still is seen,
Each change of face betrays a fault within.
If grave, 'tis spleen; he smiles but to deride;
And downright aukwardness in him is pride.
Thus must he steer through fame's uncertain seas,
Now sunk by censure, and now puff'd by praise;
Contempt with envy strangely mix'd endure,
Fear'd where caress'd, and jealous though secure.

One

One fatal rock on which good authors split
Is thinking all mankind must like their wit;
And the grand business of the world stand still
To listen to the dictates of their quill.
Hurt if they fail, and yet how few succeed!
What's born in leisure men of leisure read;
And half of those have some peculiar whim
Their test of sense, and read but to condemn.

Besides, on parties now our fame depends,
And frowns or smiles, as these are foes or friends.
Wit, judgment, nature join; you strive in vain;
'Tis keen invective stamps the current strain.
Fix'd to one side, like Homer's gods, we fight,
These always wrong, and those for ever right.
And would you chuse to see your friend, resign'd
Each conscious tie which guides the virtuous mind,
Embroil'd in factions, hurl with dreadful skill
The random vengeance of his desp'rate quill?
'Gainst pride in man with equal pride declaim,
And hide ill-nature under virtue's name?
Or deeply vers'd in flattery's wily ways,
Flow in full reams of undistinguish'd praise?
To vice's grave, or folly's bust bequeath
The blushing trophy, and indignant wreath?
^a Like Ægypt's priests, bid endless temples rise,
And people with earth's pests th' offended skies?

[a] Qui nescit qualia demens
Ægyptus portenta colat? crocodilon adorat.
    Juv. Sat. 15.

The Muse of old her native freedom knew,
And wild in air the sportive wand'rer flew;
On worth alone her bays eternal strow'd,
And found the hero, ere she hymn'd the god.
Nor less the chief his kind support return'd,
No drooping Muse her slighted labours mourn'd;
But stretch'd at ease she prun'd her growing wings,
By sages honour'd and rever'd by kings.
Ev'n knowing Greece confess'd her early claim,
And warlike Latium caught the gen'rous flame.
Not so our age regards the tuneful tongue,
'Tis senseless rapture all, and empty song:
No Pollio sheds his genial influence round,
No Varus listens whilst the groves resound.
Ev'n those, the knowing and the virtuous few,
Who noblest ends by noblest means pursue,
Forget the poet's use; the powerful spell
Of magic verse, which Sidney paints so well.
Forget that Homer wak'd the Grecian flame,
That Pindar rous'd inglorious Thebes to fame,
That every age has great examples giv'n
Of virtue taught in verse, and verse inspir'd by heav'n.

But I forbear——these dreams no longer last,
The times of fable and of flights are past.
To glory now no laurel'd suppliants bend,
No coins are struck, no sacred domes ascend.
Yet ye, who still the Muse's charms admire,
And best deserve the verse your deeds inspire,

Ev'n

Ev'n in thefe gainful unambitious days,
Feel for yourfelves at leaft, ye fond of praife,
And learn one leffon taught in myftic rhyme,
[" 'Tis verfe alone arrefts the wings of Time."
[b] Faft to the thread of life, annex'd by Fame,
A fculptur'd medal bears each human name,
O'er Lethe's ftreams the fatal threads depend,
The glitt'ring medal trembles as they bend;
Clofe but the fhears, when chance or nature calls,
The birds of rumour catch it as it falls;
Awhile from bill to bill the trifle's toft,
The waves receive it, and 'tis ever loft!

But fhould the meaneft fwan that cuts the ftream
Confign'd to Phœbus, catch the favour'd name,
Safe in her mouth fhe bears the facred prize
To where bright Fame's eternal altars rife.
'Tis there the Mufe's friends true laurels wear,
There [c] Ægypt's monarch reigns, and great Auguftus there.

Patrons of arts muft live 'till arts decay,
Sacred to verfe in every poet's lay.
Thus grateful France does Richlieu's worth proclaim,
Thus grateful Britain doats on Somers' name.
And, fpite of party rage, and human flaws,
And Britifh liberty and Britifh laws,

[b] Bacon de augmentis fcientiarum.
[c] Ptolemy Philadelphus.

Times

Times yet to come shall sing of ANNA's reign,
And bards, who blame the measures, love the men.
 But why round patrons climb th' ambitious bays?
Is interest then the sordid spur to praise?
^d Shall the same cause, which prompts the chatt'ring jay
To aim at words, inspire the poet's lay?
And is there nothing in the boasted claim
Of living labours and a deathless name?
The pictur'd front, with sacred fillets bound?
The sculptur'd bust with laurels wreath'd around?
The annual roses scatter'd o'er his urn,
And tears to flow from poets yet unborn?
 Illustrious all! but sure to merit these,
Demands at least the poet's learned ease.
Say, can the bard attempt what's truly great,
Who pants in secret for his future fate?
Him serious toils, and humbler arts engage,
To make youth easy, and provide for age;
While lost in silence hangs his useless lyre,
And though from heaven it came, fast dies the sacred fire.
Or grant true genius with superior force
Bursts every bond, resistless in its course,
Yet lives the man, how wild soe'er his aim,
Would madly barter fortune's smiles for fame?
Or distant hopes of future ease forego,
For all the wreaths that all the Nine bestow?

^d Persius.

Well

Well pleas'd to shine, through each recording page,
The hapless Dryden of a shameless age?
   Ill-fated bard! where-e'er thy name appears,
The weeping verse a sad memento bears.
Ah! what avail'd th' enormous blaze between
Thy dawn of glory, and thy closing scene!
When sinking nature asks our kind repairs,
Unstrung the nerves, and silver'd o'er the hairs;
When stay'd reflection comes uncall'd at last,
And grey experience counts each folly past,
Untun'd and harsh the sweetest strains appear,
And loudest Pæans but fatigue the ear.
   'Tis true the man of verse, though born to ills,
Too oft deserves the very fate he feels.
When, vainly frequent at the great man's board,
He shares in every vice with every lord:
Makes to their taste his sober sense submit,
And 'gainst his reason madly arms his wit;
Heav'n but in justice turns their serious heart
To scorn the wretch, whose life belies his art.
   He, only he, should haunt the Muse's grove,
Whom youth might reverence and grey hairs approve;
Whose heav'n-taught numbers, now, in thunder roll'd,
Might rouse the virtuous and appal the bold.
Now, to truth's dictates lend the grace of ease,
And teach instruction happier arts to please.
For him would PLATO change their gen'ral fate,
And own one poet might improve his state.

                                     Curs'd

Curs'd be their verse, and blasted all their bays;
Whose sensual lure th' unconscious ear betrays;
Wounds the young breast, ere virtue spreads her shield;
And takes, not wins, the scarce disputed field,
Though specious rhet'ric each loose thought refine;
Though music charm in every labour'd line,
The dangerous verse, to full perfection grown,
Bavius might blush, and Quarles disdain to own.
  Should some Machaon, whose sagacious soul,
Trac'd blushing nature to her inmost goal,
Skill'd in each drug the varying world provides,
All earth embosoms, and all ocean hides,
Nor cooling herb, nor healing balm supply,
Ease the swoln breast, or close the languid eye;
But, exquisitely ill, awake disease,
And arm with poisons every baleful breeze:
What racks, what tortures must his crimes demand,
The more than Borgia of a bleeding land!
And is less guilty he, whose shameless page
Not to the present bounds its subtile rage,
But spreads contagion wide, and stains a future age?
  Forgive me, Sir, that thus the moral strain,
With indignation warm'd, rejects the rein;
Nor think I rove regardless of my theme,
'Tis hence new dangers clog the paths to fame.
Not to themselves alone such bards confine
Fame's just reproach for virtue's injur'd shrine;

Profan'd by them, the Muse's laurels fade,
Her voice neglected, and her flame decay'd.
And the son's son must feel the father's crime;
A curse entail'd on all the race that rhyme.

New cares appear, new terrors swell the train,
And must we paint them ere we close the scene?
Say, must the Muse th' unwilling task pursue,
And to compleat her dangers mention you?
Yes you, my friend, and those whose kind regard
With partial fondness views this humble bard:
Ev'n you he dreads.——Ah! kindly cease to raise
Unwilling censure, by exacting praise.
Just to itself the jealous world will claim
A right to judge; or give, or cancel fame.
And, if th' officious zeal unbounded flows,
The friend too partial is the worst of foes.

^c Behold th' Athenian sage, whose piercing mind
Had trac'd the wily lab'rinths of mankind,
When now condemn'd, he leaves his infant care
To all those evils man is born to bear.
Not to his friends alone the charge he yields,
But nobler hopes on juster motives builds;
Bids ev'n his foes their future steps attend,
And dar'd to censure, if they dar'd offend.
Would thus the poet trust his offspring forth,
Or bloom'd our BRITAIN with ATHENIAN worth:

^c Platonis Apologia.

Would

Would the brave foe th' imperfect work engage
With honest freedom, not with partial rage,
What just productions might the world surprise!
What other POPES, what other MAROS rise!
  But since by foes, or friends alike deceiv'd,
Too little those, and these too much believ'd;
Since the same fate pursues by diff'rent ways,
Undone by censure, or undone by praise;
Since bards themselves submit to vice's rule,
And party-feuds grow high, and patrons cool:
Since, still unnam'd, unnumber'd ills behind
Rise black in air, and only wait the wind:
Let me, O let me, ere the tempest roar,
Catch the first gale, and make the nearest shore;
In sacred silence join th' inglorious train,
Where humble peace, and sweet contentment reign;
If not thy precepts, thy example own,
And steal through life not useless, though unknown.

To the Honourable Charles Townsend, Esq *;

By the Same.

O Charles, in absence hear a friend complain,
  Who knows thou lov'st him wheresoe'er he goes,
Yet feels uneasy starts of idle pain,
  And often would be told the thing he knows.
Why then, thou loiterer, fleets the silent year,
How dar'st thou give a friend unnecessary fear?

We are not now beside that osier'd stream,
  Where erst we wander'd, thoughtless of the way:
We do not now of distant ages dream,
  And cheat in converse half the ling'ring day;
No fancied heroes rise at our command,
And no Timoleon weeps, and bleeds no Theban band.

Yet why complain? thou feel'st no want like these,
  From me, 'tis true, but me alone debarr'd,
Thou still in Granta's shades enjoy'st at ease
  The books we reverenc'd, and the friends we shar'd;
Nor feest without such aids the day decline,
Nor think'st how much their loss has added weight to thine.

* Second son of Charles, the third Viscount Townsend. This accomplished gentleman, after filling some of the highest posts under government with distinguished honour, died Sept. 4, 1767, aged 42 years.

Truth's

Truth's genuine voice, the freely-opening mind,
    Are thine, are friendship's, and retirement's lot;
To conversation is the world confin'd,
    Friends of an hour, who please and are forgot;
And int'rest stains, and vanity controuls
The pure unsullied thoughts, and sallies of our souls.

    O I remember, and with pride repeat
        The rapid progress which our friendship knew!
Even at the first with willing minds we met,
    And ere the root was fix'd the branches grew.
In vain had fortune plac'd her weak barrier,
Clear was thy breast from pride, and mine from servile fear.

    I saw thee gen'rous, and with joy can say,
        My education rose above my birth,
Thanks to those parent shades, on whose cold clay
    Fall fast my tears, and lightly lie the earth!
To them I owe whate'er I dare pretend.
Thou saw'st with partial eyes, and bade me call thee friend.

    Let others meanly heap the treasur'd store,
        And aukward fondness cares on cares employ
To leave a race more exquisitely poor,
    Possess'd of riches which they ne'er enjoy:
He's only kind who takes the noble way
T' unbind the springs of thought, and give them pow'r to
        play.

His heirs shall bless him, and look down with scorn
  On vulgar pride from vaunted heroes sprung;
Lords of themselves, thank heaven that they were born
  Above the sordid miser's glitt'ring dung,
Above the servile grandeur of a throne.
For they are Nature's heirs, and all her works their own.

To Mr. GARRICK.

By the Same.

ON old PARNASSUS, t'other day,
  The Muses met to sing and play;
Apart from all the rest were seen
The tragic and the comic queen,
Engag'd, perhaps, in deep debate,
On RICH's, or on FLEETWOOD's fate.
When, on a sudden, news was brought
That GARRICK had the patent got,
And both their ladyships again
Might now return to Drury-lane.
They bow'd, they simper'd, and agreed
They wish'd the project might succeed.
'Twas very possible, the case
Was likely too, and had a face—
A-face! THALIA titt'ring cry'd,
And could her joy no longer hide;

Why,

Why, sister, all the world must see
How much this makes for you and me:
No longer now shall we expose
Our unbought goods to empty rows,
Or meanly be oblig'd to court
From foreign aid a weak support;
No more the poor polluted scene
Shall teem with births of Harlequin:
Or vindicated stage shall feel
The insults of the dancer's heel.
Such idle trash we'll kindly spare
To opera's now—they'll want them there;
For Sadler's-Wells, they say, this year
Has quite undone their engineer.

 Pugh, you're a wag, the buskin'd prude
Reply'd, and smil'd; besides 'tis rude
To laugh at foreigners, you know,
And triumph o'er a vanquish'd foe:'
For my part, I shall be content
If things succeed as they are meant;
And should not be displeas'd to find
Some changes of the tragic kind.
And say, THALIA, mayn't we hope
The stage will take a larger scope?
Shall he whose all-expressive powers
Can reach the heights that SHAKSPEARE soars,
Descend to touch an humbler key,
And tickle ears with poetry;

Where every tear is taught to flow
Through many a line's melodious woe,
And heart-felt pangs of deep distress
Are fritter'd into similes?
—O thou, whom nature taught the art,
To pierce, to cleave, to tear the heart,
Whatever name delight thine ear,
OTHELLO, RICHARD, HAMLET, LEAR,
O undertake my just defence,
And banish all but nature hence!
See, to thy aid with streaming eyes
The fair afflicted * CONSTANCE flies;
Now wild as winds in madness tears
Her heaving breasts and scatter'd hairs;
Or low on earth disdain relief,
With all the conscious pride of grief.
My PRITCHARD too in HAMLET's queen—
The goddess of the sportive vein
Here stop'd her short, and with a sneer,
My PRITCHARD, if you please, my dear!
Her tragic merit I confess,
But surely mine's her proper dress;
Behold her there with native ease,
And native spirit, born to please;
With all MARIA's charms engage,
Or MILWOOD's arts, or TOUCHWOOD's rage,
Through every foible trace the fair,
Or leave the town, and toilet's care

* Mrs. Cibber.

To chaunt in forests unconfin'd,
The wilder notes of ROSALIND.
  O thou, where'er thou fix thy praise,
BRUTE, DRUGGER, FRIBBLE, RANGER, BAYS!
O join with her in my behalf,
And teach an audience when to laugh.
So shall buffoons with shame repair
To draw in fools at Smithfield fair,
And real humour charm the age,
Though * FALSTAFF should forsake the stage.

  She spoke. MELPOMENE reply'd,
And much was said on either side;
And many a chief, and many a fair,
Were mention'd to their credit there.
But I'll not venture to display
What goddesses think fit to say.
However, GARRICK, this at least
Appears, by both a truth confess'd,
That their whole fate for many a year
But hangs on your paternal care.
A nation's taste depends on you;
—Perhaps a nation's virtue too.
O think how glorious 'twere to raise
A theatre to virtue's praise;
Where no indignant blush might rise,
Nor wit be taught to plead for vice:
But every young attentive ear
Imbibe the precepts, living there.

* Mr. Quin, inimitable in that character, who was then leaving the

And

And every unexperienc'd breast
There feel its own rude hints express'd,
And, waken'd by the glowing scene,
Unfold the worth that lurks within.

If possible, be perfect quite;
A few short rules will guide you right,
Consult your own good sense in all,
Be deaf to fashion's fickle call,
Nor e'er descend from reason's laws
To court what you command, applause.

NATURE to Dr. HOADLY,
On his Comedy of the SUSPICIOUS HUSBAND.
By the Same.

SLY hypocrite! was this your aim?
To borrow Pæon's sacred name,
And lurk beneath his graver mien,
To trace the secrets of my reign?
Did I for this applaud your zeal,
And point out each minuter wheel,
Which finely taught the next to roll,
And made my works one perfect whole?
For who, but I, 'till you appear'd
To model the dramatic herd,
E'er bade to wond'ring ears and eyes,
Such pleasing intricacies rise?

Where

Where every part is nicely true,
Yet touches still some master clue;
Each riddle opening by degrees,
'Till all unravels with such ease,
That only those who will be blind
Can feel one doubt perplex their mind.

   Nor was't enough, you thought, to write,
But you must impiously unite
With GARRICK too, who long before
Had stole my whole expressive pow'r.
That changeful Proteus of the stage
Usurps my mirth, my grief, my rage;
And as his diff'rent parts incline,
Gives joys or pains, sincere as mine.

   Yet you shall find (howe'er elate
You triumph in your former cheat)
'Tis not so easy to escape
In Nature's as in Pæon's shape.
For every critic, great or small,
Hates every thing that's natural.
The beaus, and ladies too, can say,
What does he mean? is this a play?
We see such people every day.
Nay more, to chafe, and teaze your spleen,
And teach you how to steal again,
My very fools shall prove you're bit,
And damn you for your want of wit.

The Youth and the Philosopher.

A FABLE.

By the Same.

A Grecian Youth, of talents rare,
Whom Plato's philosophic care
Had form'd for virtue's nobler view,
By precept and example too,
Would often boaſt his matchleſs ſkill,
To curb the ſteed, and guide the wheel.
And as he paſs'd the gazing throng,
With graceful eaſe, and ſmack'd the thong,
The ideot wonder they expreſs'd
Was praiſe and tranſport to his breaſt.

At length quite vain, he needs would ſhew
His maſter what his art could do;
And bade his ſlaves the chariot lead
To Academus' ſacred ſhade.
The trembling grove confeſs'd its fright,
The wood nymphs ſtarted at the ſight,
The Muſes drop the learned lyre,
And to their inmoſt ſhades retire!

'Howe'er, the youth with forward air,
Bows to the ſage, and mounts the car,

The

The lash resounds, the coursers spring,
The chariot marks the rolling ring,
And gath'ring crowds with eager eyes,
And shouts, pursue him as he flies.

Triumphant to the goal return'd,
With nobler thirst his bosom burn'd;
And now along th' indented plain,
The self-same track he marks again,
Pursues with care the nice design,
Nor ever deviates from the line.

Amazement seiz'd the circling crowd;
The youths with emulation glow'd;
Ev'n bearded sages hail'd the boy,
And all, but Plato, gaz'd with joy.
For he, deep-judging sage, beheld
With pain the triumphs of the field:
And when the charioteer drew nigh,
And, flush'd with hope, had caught his eye,
Alas! unhappy youth, he cry'd,
Expect no praise from me, (and sigh'd)
With indignation I survey
Such skill and judgment thrown away.
The time profusely squander'd there,
On vulgar arts beneath thy care,
If well employ'd, at less expence,
Had taught thee honour, virtue, sense,
And rais'd thee from a coachman's fate
To govern men, and guide the state.

Aa

An ODE to a GENTLEMAN;
On his pitching a Tent in his GARDEN.
By the Same.

AH! friend, forbear, nor fright the fields
    With hostile scenes of imag'd war;
Content still roves the blooming wilds,
    And sheds her mildest influence there:
Ah! drive not the sweet wand'rer from her seat,
Nor with rude arts profane her latest best retreat.

    Are there not bowers, and sylvan scenes,
        By nature's kind luxuriance wove?
    Has Romely * lost the living greens
        Which erst adorn'd her artless grove?
Where through each hallow'd haunt the poet stray'd,
And met the willing Muse, and peopled every shade.

    But now no bards thy woods among,
        Shall wait th' inspiring Muse's call;
    For though to mirth and festal song
        Thy choice devotes the woven wall,
Yet what avails that all be peace within,
If horrors guard the gate, and scare us from the scene?

    'Tis true of old the patriarch spread
        His happier tents which knew not war,
    And chang'd at will the trampled mead
        For fresher greens and purer air;

    * In Scarsdale, in the County of Derby.

But long has man forgot such simple ways,
Truth unsuspecting harm!—the dream of ancient days.

   Ev'n he, cut off from human kind,
     (Thy neighb'ring wretch) the child of Care,
   Who, to his native mines confin'd,
     Nor sees the sun, nor breathes the air,
But 'midst the damps and darkness of earth's womb
Drags out laborious life, and scarcely dreads the tomb;

   Ev'n he, should some indulgent chance
     Transport him to thy sylvan reign,
   Would eye the floating veil askance,
     And hide him in his caves again,
While dire presage in every breeze that blows
Hears shrieks and clashing arms, and all Germania's woes.

   And doubt not thy polluted taste
     A sudden vengeance shall pursue;
   Each fairy form we whilom trac'd
     Along the morn or evening dew,
Nymph, Satyr, Faun, shall vindicate their grove,
Robb'd of its genuine charms, and hospitable Jove.

   I see, all-arm'd with dews unblest,
     Keen frosts, and noisome vapours drear,
   Already, from the bleak north-east,
     The Genius of the wood appear!

—Far

—Far other office once his prime delight,
To nurse thy saplings tall, and heal the harms of night.

   With ringlets quaint to curl thy shade,
     To bid the insect tribes retire,
   To guard thy walks and not invade——
     O wherefore then provoke his ire?
   Alas! with prayers, with tears his rage repel,
While yet the red'ning shoots with embryo-blossoms swell.

   Too late thou'lt weep, when blights deform
     The fairest produce of the year;
   Too late thou'lt weep, when every storm
     Shall loudly thunder in thy ear,
   " Thus, thus the green-hair'd deities maintain
" Their own eternal rights, and Nature's injur'd reign."

On a MESSAGE-CARD in Verse,
Sent by a LADY.
By the Same.

HERMES, the gamester of the sky,
   To share for once mankind's delights,
Slip'd down to earth, exceeding sly,
   And bade his coachman drive to White's.
In form a beau; so light he trips,
   You'd swear his wings were at his heels;
From glass to glass alert he skips,
   And bows and prattles while he deals.

In short, so well his part he play'd,
    The waiters took him for a peer;
And ev'n some great ones whisp'ring said
    He was no vulgar foreigner.
Whate'er he was, he swept the board,
    Won every bett and every game;
Stript even the Rooks, who stampt and roar'd,
    And wonder'd how the devil it came!
He wonder'd too, and thought it hard;
    But found at last this great command
Was owing to one fav'rite card,
    Which still brought luck into his hand.
The four of spades, whene'er he saw
    Its sable spots, he laugh'd at rules,
Took odds beyond the gaming law,
    And Hoyle * and Philidor were fools.
But now, for now 'twas time to go,
    What gratitude shall he express?
And what peculiar boon bestow
    Upon the cause of his success?
Suppose, for something must be done,
    On Juno's self he could prevail
To pick the pips out, one by one,
    And stick them in her peacock's tail.

---

* Of these well-known calculators, whose works are more than sufficiently studied, it is enough to observe, that one wrote on the Game at Whist, and the other on that of Chess.

Should Pallas have it, was a doubt,
  To twift her filk, or range her pins;
Or fhould the Mufes cut it out,
  For bridges to their violins.
To Venus fhould the prize be given,
  Superior beauty's juft reward,
And 'gainft the next great rout in heaven
  Be fent her for a meffage-card.
Or hold—by Jove, a lucky hit!
  Your goddeffes are arrant farces;
Go, carry it to Mrs. ——
  And bid her fill it full of verfes.

The *Je ne fçai Quoi*. A SONG.

By the Same.

I.

YES, I'm in love, I feel it now,
  And CÆLIA has undone me!
And yet I'll fwear I can't tell how
  The pleafing plague ftole on me.

II.

'Tis not her face which love creates,
  For there no graces revel;
'Tis not her fhape, for there the fates
  Have rather been uncivil.

III.

'Tis not her air, for sure in that
   There's nothing more than common;
And all her sense is only chat,
   Like any other woman.

IV.

Her voice, her touch might give th' alarm—
   'Twas both perhaps, or neither;
In short, 'twas that provoking charm
   Of CÆLIA altogether.

An ODE

On a distant Prospect of

ETON COLLEGE.

Written in 1742.

By Mr. GRAY [a].

YE distant spires, ye antique towers,
   That crown the wat'ry glade,
Where grateful science still adores
   Her HENRY's [b] holy shade;   And

---

[a] Thomas Gray, the son of Mr. Philip Gray, a scrivener of London, was born Nov. 26, 1716. His grammatical education he received as Eton, under Mr. Antrobus, his mother's brother; and when he left school,

And ye that from the stately brow
Of WINDSOR's heights th' expanse below
Of grove, of lawn, of mead survey,
Whose turf, whose shade, whose flowers among
Wanders the hoary Thames along
His silver-winding way.

 Ah happy hills, ah pleasing shade,
Ah fields belov'd in vain,
Where once my careless childhood stray'd,
A stranger yet to pain!

school, in 1734, entered a pensioner at Peter-house in Cambridge. After continuing there about five years, he accepted an invitation from his school-fellow, Mr. Horace Walpole, to accompany him on his travels. They accordingly visited France and Italy together; but a difference arising between them, they separated, and Mr. Gray returned to England alone. Soon afterwards he lost his father, who left him in circumstances so narrow, that he found himself obliged to relinquish the study of the law, to which he had proposed to devote himself, and retire to Cambridge, where he resided, with only one interval, during the rest of his life. The college which he first made choice of was Peter-house; but being offended at some liberties taken with him by a few young men in that society, he removed in 1756 to Pembroke College. In 1762 he applied for the professorship of modern languages without success, but obtained it in 1768 without any solicitation. He had some time been afflicted with the gout, a disorder which, in spite of the most rigid temperance, gained ground upon his constitution, and in the end falling upon his stomach, put a period to his life, July 30, 1771. His character, both as a writer and a man, is sufficiently known from the lives of him by Mr. Mason and Dr. Johnson.

 b King Henry VIth, founder of the college.

               I feel

I feel the gales, that from ye blow,
A momentary bliſs beſtow,
As waving freſh their gladſome wing,
My weary ſoul they ſeem to ſooth,
And, redolent [c] of joy and youth,
To breathe a ſecond ſpring.

 Say, father THAMES, for thou haſt ſeen
Full many a ſprightly race
Diſporting on thy margent green,
The paths of pleaſure trace,
Who foremoſt now delight to cleave
With pliant arms thy glaſſy wave?
The captive linnet which enthrall?
What idle progeny ſucceed
To chaſe the rolling circle's ſpeed,
Or urge the flying ball?

 While ſome on earneſt buſineſs bent
Their murm'ring labours ply,
'Gainſt graver hours, that bring conſtraint
To ſweeten liberty:
Some bold adventurers diſdain
The limits of their little reign,

[c] IMITATION.

And bees their honey redolent of ſpring.
   Dryden's Fable on the Pythag. Syſtem.

And unknown regions dare defcry:
Still as they run, they look behind,
They hear a voice in every wind,
And fnatch a fearful joy.

   Gay hope is theirs by fancy fed,
Lefs pleafing when poffefs'd;
The tear forgot as foon as fhed,
The fun-fhine of the breaft.
Theirs buxom health of rofy hue,
Wild wit, invention ever-new,
And lively chear of vigour born:
The thoughtlefs day, the eafy night,
The fpirits pure, the flumbers light,
That fly th' approach of morn

   Alas, regardlefs of their doom,
The little victims play!
No fenfe have they of ills to come,
No care beyond to-day:
Yet fee how all around 'em wait
The minifters of human fate,
And black misfortune's baleful train!
Ah! fhew them where in ambufh ftand,
To feize their prey, the murth'rous band!
Ah! fhew them they are men!

   Thefe fhall the fury paffions tear,
The vultures of the mind,
Difdainful anger, pallid fear,
And fhame that fculks behind;

                                            Or

Or pining love shall waste their youth,
Or jealousy with rankling tooth,
That inly gnaws the secret heart,
And envy wan, and faded care,
Grim-visag'd comfortless despair,
And sorrow's piercing dart.

Ambition this shall tempt to rise,
Then whirl the wretch from high,
To bitter scorn a sacrifice,
And grinning infamy;
The stings of falshood those shall try,
And hard unkindness' alter'd eye [d],
That mocks the tear it forc'd to flow;
And keen remorse with blood defil'd,
And moody madness laughing wild [e]
Amidst severest woe.

[d] "The elision here (says Mr. Mason) is ungraceful, and hurts this otherwise beautiful line: One of the same kind (in the second line of the next Ode) makes the same blemish; but I think they are the only two to be found in this correct writer; and I mention them here, that succeeding Poets may not look upon them as authorities. The judicious reader will not suppose, that I would condemn all elisions of the genitive case, by this stricture on those which are terminated by rough consonants. Many there are which the ear readily admits, and which use has made familiar to it."

[e] IMITATION,

—— Madness laughing in her ireful mood.

Dryden's Palamon and Arcite.

  Lo, in the vale of years beneath,
A grisly troop are seen,
The painful family of death,
More hideous than their queen;
This racks the joints, this fires the veins,
That every lab'ring sinew strains,
Those in the deeper vitals rage;
Lo, poverty, to fill the band,
That numbs the soul with icy hand,
And slow-consuming age.

  To each his suff'rings: all are men,
Condemn'd alike to groan,
The tender for another's pain;
Th' unfeeling for his own.
Yet ah! why should they know their fate!
Since sorrow never comes too late,
And happiness too swiftly flies.
Thought would destroy their paradise.
No more; where ignorance is bliss,
'Tis folly to be wise.

O D E.

ODE.

Written in 1742.
By the Same.

I.

LO! where the rosy-bosom'd hours,
   Fair VENUS' train appear,
Disclose the long-expecting flowers,
And wake the purple year!
The ATTIC warbler pours her throat
Responsive to the cuckow's note,
The untaught harmony of spring:
While whisp'ring pleasure as they fly,
Cool Zephyrs through the clear blue sky
Their gathered fragrance fling.

II.

Where'er the oak's thick branches stretch
A broader, browner shade;
Where'er the rude and moss-green beech
O'er-canopies the glade [a];

---

[a] IMITATION.
———a bank
O'er-canopied with luscious woodbine.
                Shakspeare's Midf. Nights Dream.

Beside some water's rushy brink
With me the Muse shall sit and think
(At ease reclin'd in rustic state)
How vain the ardour of the crowd,
How low, how little are the proud,
How indigent the great [b] !

III.

Still is the toiling hand of care:
The panting herds repose:
Yet hark, how through the peopled air
The busy murmur glows!
The insect youth are on the wing,
Eager to taste the honied spring,
And float amid the liquid noon [c]:
Some lightly o'er the current skim,

[b] VARIATION.

  How low, how indigent the proud;
  How little are the great.

Thus it stood in the former editions of this work, where it was first published. "The Author (says Mr. Mason) corrected it, on account "of the point of *little* and *great*. It certainly had too much the ap- "pearance of a concetto, though it expressed his meaning better than "the present reading."

[c] IMITATION.

  Nare per æstatem liquidam.
       Virgil, Georg. lib. 4.

Some shew their gayly-gilded trim
Quick-glancing to the sun [d].

IV.

To Contemplation's sober eye [e]
Such is the race of man:
And they that creep, and they that fly,
Shall end where they began.
Alike the busy and the gay
But flutter through life's little day,
In fortune's varying colours dress'd:
Brush'd by the hand of rough mischance,
Or chill'd by age, their airy dance
They leave, in dust to rest.

V.

Methinks I hear in accents low
The sportive kind reply:
Poor moralist! and what art thou?
A solitary fly!
Thy joys no glittering female meets,
No hive hast thou of hoarded sweets,

---

[d] IMITATION.

———Sporting with quick glance,
Shew to the sun their wav'd coats dropt with gold.
Milton's Par. Lost, b. vii.

[e] IMITATION.

While insects from the threshold preach, &c.
See *The Grotto,* by Matthew Green, vol. v. p. 174.

No painted plumage to display:
On hasty wings thy youth is flown;
Thy sun is set, thy spring is gone—
We frolic, while 'tis May.

ODE on the Death of a Favourite CAT, Drowned in a Tub[a] of Gold Fishes.

Written in 1747.

By the Same.

I.

'TWAS on a lofty vase's side,
　Where China's gayest art had dy'd
The azure flowers, that blow;
Demurest of the Tabby kind,
The pensive Selima reclin'd,
　Gaz'd on the lake below.

II.

Her conscious tail her joy declar'd;
The fair round face, the snowy beard,

---

[a] The vase, not tub, in which Mr. Walpole's cat was drowned is now at Strawberry Hill, with this legend—
　"'Twas on *this* lofty vase's side," &c.

The

The velvet of her paws,
The coat that with the tortoise vies,
Her ears of jet, and emerald eyes,
    She saw; and purr'd applause.

III.

Still had she gaz'd: but 'midst the tide
Two angel forms [b] were seen to glide,
    The Genii of the stream;
Their scaly armour's Tyrian hue
Through richest purple to the view
    Betray'd a golden gleam.

IV.

The hapless nymph with wonder saw:
A whisker first, and then a claw,
    With many an ardent wish,
She stretch'd in vain to reach the prize.
What female heart can gold despise?
    What cat's averse to fish?

V.

Presumptuous maid! with looks intent
Again she stretch'd, again she bent,
    Nor knew the gulph between;
(Malignant Fate sat by and smil'd)
The slipp'ry verge her feet beguil'd,
    She tumbled headlong in.

---

[b] Two beauteous forms.—First Edition.

VI.

Eight times emerging from the flood
She mew'd to every wat'ry god,
  Some speedy aid to send.
No Dolphin came, no Nereid stirr'd:
Nor cruel Tom, nor Susan heard,
  A fav'rite has no friend!

VII.

From hence, ye beauties undeceiv'd,
Know, one false step is ne'er retriev'd,
  And be with caution bold.
Not all that tempts your wand'ring eyes
And heedless hearts, is lawful prize;
  Nor all, that glisters, gold.

A MONODY
On the DEATH of
Queen CAROLINE.

By RICHARD WEST [a], Esq; Son to the Chancellor of Ireland, and Grandson to Bishop BURNET.

I.

SING we no more of HYMENEAL lays,
  Nor strew the land with myrtles and with bays:
The voice of joy is fled the BRITISH shore,
For CAROLINE's no more: And

---

[a] This young gentleman, who was educated at Eton, and Christ Church Oxford, was the intimate friend of Mr. Gray and Mr. Horace Walpole.

And now our forrows afk a fadder ftring;
Come, plaintive goddefs of the Cyrrhan fpring,
Pour thy deep note, and fhed thy tuneful tear,
And, while we lofe the memory of pain
In thy oblivious ftrain,
——Ah! drop thy cyprefs on yon mournful bier!
Begin: nor more delay
The facred meed of gratitude to pay:
Begin: whate'er immortal fong can do,
To the dear name of CAROLINE is due:
Who loves the Mufe, deferves the Mufe's love:
Then raife thy numbers high,
Sound out her glory to the throne of Jove,
Spread the glad voice through all the ambient fky,
From the dull marble vindicate her praife,
And waft it down to lighten future days.

II.

Ye bards to come, the fong of truth attend:
This, this is fhe, the Mufe's judge and friend!
The royal female! whofe benignant hand
Throughout fair ALBION's land
Dealt every ufeful, every decent part,
Each MEMPHIAN fcience, and each ATTIC art:
Within the Mufe's bower,
She oft was wont to lofe the vacant hour,

He was intended for the profeffion of the Law, but declined the purfuit partly from a diflike of it, and partly from ill health. He died at Pope's, in Hatfield, of a confumption, 1 June 1742, in the 26th year of his age.

Or

Or underneath the sapient grot reclin'd,
Her soul to contemplation she resign'd,
And for a while laid down
The painful, envied burthen of a crown :
Mean time thy rural ditty was not mute,
Sweet bard of MERLIN's cave [b] !
Though rude, the ditty was of her, who gave
Thy voice to sing, and tun'd thy oaten flute
In strains unwonted to the ear of swain :
As when the lark, ambitious of the skies,
Quits the low harvest of the golden plain,
Taught by the sun's inspiring warmth to rise,
Sublime in air he spreads his dappled wings,
Mounts the blue æther, and in mounting sings.

III.

But whither wanders the licentious song ?
Such joyous notes to happier days belong !
Ah me ! our happier days are now no more :—
Return, sad Muse : see pale BRITANNIA weep,
See all the sisters of the subject deep
Their sovereign's loss deplore !
See fond IERNE gives her sorrows vent,
And as she tunes her brazen lyre to woe,
Indulge her grief to flow !—
See even the northern ORCADES lament !

---

[b] Stephen Duck, who was patronized by the Queen, and had been appointed keeper of Merlin's cave in Richmond Park.

Nor ends the wailing here:
Where'er beneath our flag wild Ocean roars,
From fartheſt ORIENT to HESPERIA's ſhores,
From torrid AFRIC to the world's cold end,
The BRITISH woes extend,
And every colony has dropt a tear.

IV.

O honour'd flood! with reeds Pierian crown'd,
ISIS! whoſe argent waters glide along
Fair BELLOSITE's Lycæan-ſhades renown'd,
Now aid my feeble ſong;
And call thy choſen ſons, and bid them bring
Their lays of DORIC air,
With lenient ſounds to ſteal awhile from care
Th' inconſolable King:
O! ſooth his anguiſh, and compoſe his pains
With artful unimaginable ſtrains,
According ſweetly to the golden lyre,
Such as might half inſpire
The iron breaſt of HADES to reſign
Our loſt, lov'd CAROLINE.

V.

Theſe are thy glorious deeds, almighty Death!
Theſe are thy triumphs o'er the ſons of men,
That now receive the miſerable breath,
Which the next moment they reſign again!
Ah me! what boots us all our boaſted power,
Our golden treaſure, and our purpled ſtate?
They cannot ward th' inevitable hour,
Nor ſtay the fearful violence of Fate:

—Virtue

—Virtue herself shall fail :
Else now, if virtue ever could prevail,
Death had not dar'd to violate the throne,
Nor had BRITANNIA heard her sovereign groan.
—Ye nymphs ! recall the song :
For heaven-born virtue does to heaven belong,
And scorns the meanest of her sons should die,
But opens him a passage to the sky ;
Her rod ay pointing to the eternal goal,
From the brute earth she frees the ardent soul ;
Swift from the vulgar herd aloft she springs,
Spurns the moist clay, and soars on azure wings.

VI.

Then hence with sorrows vain :
Ye Theban Muses ! elevate the strain :
Search o'er the records of immortal fame,
And high refu'gent on the female line,
Imblaze in starry characters the name
Of BRITISH CAROLINE :
While sacred story rings with SHEBA's praise,
While BERENICE's virtues still inspire
The CYRENEAN lyre,
And GLORIANA blooms in Spenser's lays ;
Thy name, great Queen, shall glow in every page,
Shall dwell in every clime, and live in every age.
When GEORGE shall go, where WILLIAM went before,
And all the present world shall be no more ;

When

When the fond factions of unjuſt mankind,
The mean, the mad, the envious, and the blind,
Shall turn to worms and duſt;
Then Time, impartial judge, that ſtates the price
Of each man's virtue, and of each man's vice,
From thy bright fame ſhall clear the cank'ring ruſt;
And O! the Muſes ever ſhall be juſt.

VII.

But lo! what ſudden radiance gilds the ſkies?
'Tis Gratitude deſcending from above,
Known by the ſweetneſs of her dove-like eyes,
Daughter of truth and univerſal love!
To HENRY's ſacred dome ſhe wafts along,
And on thy tomb ſhe pours
Celeſtial ſweets and amaranthine flowers:
The old, the young, the rich, the wretched crowd
Numerous around her, and with accents loud
Raiſe the mix'd voice, and pour the grateful ſong:
" Hail Queen! adorn'd by nature and by art!
" Thine was each virtue of the head and heart;
" Thy people bleſt thee, and thy children lov'd,
" And thy King honour'd, and thy God approv'd."

VIII.

But here my labours ceaſe:
'Tis time the foaming courſer to releaſe.
And thou, O royal ſhade,
Forgive the Muſe, that theſe vain honours paid;

A Muſe

A Muse as yet unheeded and unknown;
That dares to sacrifice to truth alone,
Not prone to blame, nor hasty to commend,
No foe unjust, no mercenary friend,
No sensual bosom, no ungenerous mind,
And though not virtuous, virtuously inclin'd.

A PIPE

A PIPE of TOBACCO:

In Imitation of

Six Several AUTHORS.

By ISAAC HAWKINS BROWNE, Esq*.

IMITATION I.—COLLEY CIBBER.

A NEW-YEAR'S ODE.

Laudes egregii Cæsaris——
Culpa deterere ingeni.   HOR.

RECITATIVO.

OLD battle-array, big with horror is fled,
  And olive-rob'd peace again lifts up her head.
Sing, ye Muses, TOBACCO, the blessing of peace;
Was ever a nation so blessed as this?

AIR.

---

* Isaac Hawkins Browne was born at Burton upon Trent, 21 January 1705-6. He received his grammatical education first at Litchfield

A I R.

When summer suns grow red with heat,
 Tobacco tempers Phœbus' ire,
When wintry storms around us beat,
 Tobacco cheers with gentle fire.
  Yellow autumn, youthful spring,
  In thy praises jointly sing.

and then at Westminster, where he was equally distinguished for the brilliancy of his parts and the steadiness of his application. When he was little more than sixteen years of age he was removed to Trinity College, Cambridge, where he remained until he had taken his degree of Master of Arts. In May 1724, King George the First established at both universities a foundation for the study of modern history and languages, with the design of qualifying young men for employments at court, and foreign embassies. On this foundation Mr. Browne was selected as one of the first scholars. About 1727 he settled at Lincoln's Inn, and was called to the Bar, at which he continued several years; but never arrived at any eminence in the practical part of his profession. He was twice chosen member of Parliament for the borough of Wenlock in Shropshire, and died 14 February 1760, in the 55th year of his age. The idea of the above imitations was first suggested by Dr. John Hoadly, who was the author of the first of them, though it afterwards received so much alteration from Mr. Browne, that he had fairly made it his own, as the Dr. used to acknowledge.

RECITATIVO.

Like NEPTUNE, CÆSAR guards VIRGINIAN fleets;
  Fraught with TOBACCO's balmy sweets;
Old Ocean trembles at BRITANNIA's power,
  And BOREAS is afraid to roar.

AIR.

Happy mortal! he who knows
Pleasure which a PIPE bestows:
Curling eddies climb the room,
Wafting round a mild perfume.

RECITATIVO.

Let foreign climes the wine and orange boast,
While wastes of war deform the teeming coast;
BRITANNIA, distant from each hostile sound,
Enjoys a PIPE, with ease and freedom crown'd;
E'en restless faction finds itself most free,
Or if a slave, a slave to liberty.

AIR.

Smilling years that gayly run
Round the zodiac with the sun,
Tell, if ever you have seen
Realms so quiet and serene.
BRITISH sons no longer now
Hurl the bar, or twang the bow,
Nor of crimson combat think,
But securely smoke and drink.

T 4   CHORUS.

CHORUS.

Smiling years, that gayly run
Round the zodiac with the sun,
Tell, if ever you have seen
Realms so quiet and serene.

IMITATION II.——Amb. Philips.

Tenues fugit ceu fumus in auras.   Virg.

LITTLE tube of mighty pow'r,
Charmer of an idle hour,
Object of my warm desire,
Lip of wax, and eye of fire:
And thy snowy taper waist,
With my finger gently brac'd;
And thy pretty swelling crest,
With my little stopper prest,
And the sweetest bliss of blisses,
Breathing from thy balmy kisses.
Happy thrice, and thrice agen,
Happiest he of happy men;
Who when agen the night returns,
When agen the taper burns,
When agen the cricket's gay,
(Little cricket, full of play)
Can afford his tube to feed
With the fragrant Indian weed:

Pleasure

Pleasure for a nose divine,
Incense of the god of wine.
Happy thrice, and thrice agen,
Happiest he of happy men.

IMITATION III.——JAMES THOMSON.

*——Prorumpit ad æthera nubem
Turbine, fumantem piceo.*   VIRG.

O Thou, matur'd by glad Hesperian suns,
   TOBACCO, fountain pure of [a] *limpid truth,*
That looks the very soul; whence pouring thought
Swarms all the mind; absorpt is yellow care,
[b] *And at each puff imagination burns:*
Flash on thy bard, and with exalting fires
Touch the mysterious lip, that chaunts thy praise
In strains to mortal sons of earth unknown.
Behold an engine, wrought from tawny mines
Of ductile clay, with [c] *plastic virtue* form'd,
And glaz'd magnific o'er, I grasp, I fill.
From PÆTOTHEKE [d] with pungent pow'rs perfum'd;
[e] *Itself one tortoise all, where shines imbib'd
Each parent ray;* then rudely ramm'd illume,

---

[a] Poem on Liberty, ver. 12.   [b] Ibid. ver. 16.   [c] Ibid. ver. 104.
[d] A poetical word for a tobacco-box.   [e] Poem on Liberty,
ver. 243, 245.

With the red touch of zeal-enkindling sheet;
f Mark'd with Gibsonian lore; forth issue clouds,
Thought-thrilling, thirst-inciting clouds around,
And many-mining fires; I all the while,
Lolling at ease, g *inhale* the breezy balm.
But chief, when *Bacchus wont with thee to join,*
In genial strife and orthodoxal ale,
h *Stream life and joy into the Muse's bowl.*
Oh be thou still *my great inspirer*, thou
My Muse; oh fan me with thy zephyrs boon,
While I, in clouded tabernacle shrin'd,
Burst forth all oracle and mystic song.

IMITATION IV.——Dr. Young.

—— Bullatis mihi nugis
Pagina turgescat—dare pondus idonea fumo. Pers.

CRITICS avaunt! Tobacco is my theme;
Tremble like hornets at the blasting steam.
And you, court-insects, flutter not too near
Its light, nor buzz within the scorching sphere.
Pollio, with flame like thine, my verse inspire,
So shall the Muse from smoke elicit fire.
Coxcombs prefer the tickling sting of snuff;
Yet all their claim to wisdom is —— a puff:

---

f Poem on Liberty, ver. 247, alluding to the pastoral letters of Bishop Gibson.   g Ibid. ver. 309.   h Ibid. ver. 171.

Lord FOPLIN smokes not——for his teeth afraid:
Sir TAWDRY smokes not——for he wears brocade.
Ladies, when pipes are brought, affect to swoon;
They love no smoke, except the smoke of town;
But courtiers hate the puffing tribe,——no matter,
Strange if they love the breath that cannot flatter!
Its foes but shew their ignorance; can he
Who scorns the leaf of knowledge, love the tree?
The tainted Templar (more prodigious yet)
Rails at TOBACCO, though it makes him——spit.
CITRONIA vows it has an odious stink;
She will not smoke (ye gods!)—but she will drink:
And chaste PRUDELLA (blame her if you can),
Says, pipes are us'd by that vile creature Man:
Yet crowds remain, who still its worth proclaim,
While some for pleasure smoke, and some for fame:
Fame, of our actions universal spring,
For which we drink, eat, sleep, smoke—every thing.

IMITATION V.——MR. POPE.

———— *Solis ad ortus*
Vanescit fumus.   LUCAN.

BLEST leaf! whose aromatic gales dispense
   To templars modesty, to parsons sense:
So raptur'd priests, at fam'd DODONA's shrine
Drank inspiration from the steam divine.
Poison that cures, a vapour that affords
Content, more solid than the smile of lords:

Rest

Reft to the weary, to the hungry food,
The laft kind refuge of the WISE and GOOD.
Infpir'd by thee, dull cits adjuft the fcale
Of Europe's peace, when other ftatefmen fail.
By thee protected, and thy fifter, beer,
Poets rejoice, nor think the bailiff near.
Nor lefs the critic owns thy genial aid,
While fupperlefs he plies the piddling trade.
What though to love and foft delights a foe,
By ladies hated, hated by the beau,
Yet focial freedom, long to courts unknown,
Fair health, fair truth, and virtue are thy own.
Come to thy poet, come with healing wings,
And let me tafte thee unexcis'd by kings.

IMITATION VI.——DEAN SWIFT.

Ex fumo dare lucem. HOR.

BOY! bring an ounce of FREEMAN's beft,
And bid the vicar be my gueft:
Let all be plac'd in manner due,
A pot wherein to fpit or fpue,
And London Journal, and Free-Briton*,
Of ufe to light a pipe or * *
* * * * * * * * *
* * * * * * * * *

This village, unmolefted yet
By troopers, fhall be my retreat:

* Two minifterial news-papers.

Who cannot flatter, bribe, betray;
Who cannot write or vote for *.
Far from the vermin of the town,
Here let me rather live, my own,
Doze o'er a pipe, whose vapour bland
In sweet oblivion lulls the land;
Of all which at Vienna passes,
As ignorant as * * Brass is:
And scorning rascals to caress,
Extol the days of good Queen BESS,
When first TOBACCO blest our isle,
Then think of other Queens——and smile.

 Come, jovial pipe, and bring along
 Midnight revelry and song;
 The merry catch, the madrigal,
 That echoes sweet in City Hall;
 The parson's pun, the smutty tale
 Of country justice o'er his ale.
 I ask not what the French are doing,
 Or Spain, to compass Britain's ruin:
  Britons, if undone, can go,
  Where TOBACCO loves to grow.

ODE

ODE to the Hon. Charles Yorke[a], Esq.

By the Same.

CHARLES, son of Yorke, who on the mercy-seat
Of justice states the bounds of right and wrong;
    Not like the vulgar law-bewilder'd throng,
Who in the maze of error, hope to meet
Truth, or hope rather to delude with lies
And airy phantoms, under truth's disguise.

Some wrapt in precedents, or points decreed,
    Or lop or stretch the laws to forms precise;
    Some, who the pedantry of rules despise,
Plain sense adopt, from legal fetters freed;
Sense without science, fleeting, unconfin'd,
Is empty guess, and shifts with every wind.

But he, thy sire, with more discerning toil,
    Rang'd the wide field, sagacious to explore
    Where lay dispers'd or hid the precious ore;
Then form'd into a whole the gather'd spoil,
Law, reason, equity, which now unite,
Reflecting each on each a friendly light.

[a] Afterwards Lord High Chancellor of Great Britain. He died 22d of January 1770.

Blest in a guide, a pattern so compleat,
    Tread, as thou do'st, his footsteps; for not rude
    Thy genius, not uncultur'd, unsubdu'd.
Yet there are intervals, and seasons meet,
To smooth the brow of thought; nor thou disdain
Fit hour of vacance with the Muse's train.

Let meaner spirits, cast in common mould,
    Who feed on husks of learned lore, refuse
    To hear the lessons of the warbling Muse;
Nor know that bards, the lawgivers of old,
By soothing song to moral truth beguil'd
Man, 'till then fierce, a lawless race, and wild.

What means the lyre, by which the fabled sage
    Drew beasts to listen, and made rocks advance
    Around him as he play'd, in mystic dance?
What, but the Muse? who soften'd human rage,
Parent of concord, she prepar'd the plan
Of social life, and man attun'd to man.

She taught the sphéres to move in fair array,
    Each in their orbits heark'ning to her strain;
    Else would they wander o'er th' etherial plain
Licentious, but that she directs their way:
She aw'd to temper, by her magic spell,
The warring elements, and powers of hell.

They err, who think the MUSES not ally'd
   To THEMIS; both are of celestial birth:
     Both give peace, order, harmony to earth;
Both by one heav'nly fountain are supply'd;
And men and angels hymn, in general quire,
What law ordains, and what the NINE inspire.

From CÆLIA to CLOE.

By the Same.

I Rural life enjoy, the town's your taste,
  In this we differ, twins in all the rest.
Yet when the dog-star brings diseases on,
And each fond mother trembles for her son;
Now when the Mall's forlorn, the beaux and belles
All for retirement crowd to Tunbridge-Wells;
Say, will not CLOE for awhile withdraw
From dear Vaux-hall and charming Ranelagh?
Sure at this homely hut one may contrive
Awhile not only to exist, but live;
For not dull landscapes here my thoughts engross,
Woods, lawns, and rills, and grottoes green with moss.

                                            No,

No, the fame appetite that courts infuse,
Haunts in retreat, and to the shade pursues.
Here all my cares are to receive and pay
Visits, my studies a romance or play:
And then to pass the live-long Sunday off,
Walks or a ride, nay church serves well enough;
At church; one has a chance to see cockades,
Lur'd thither in pursuit of country maids:
Or tall Hibernian smit with fond desire
To wed the only daughter of a squire.
Cards have their turn, to kill a tedious hour;
If baulk'd of whist, piquette is in my pow'r;
For oft the captain, fresh from town, bestows
A friendly week upon his friend my spouse.
Then gaily glide the days on downy feet,
For sure the captain has prodigious wit;
O I could hear his sweet discourse for ever,
Of all that's done, and who and who's together.
Oft far and wide for new delights I range,
True sex, and constant to the love of change.
Is there within ten miles a troop review'd,
An auction of old goods, an interlude
By strolling players, an horse-race, or a ball?
There to be seen I have an urgent call.
The labours of the plough are then forgot,
And THOMAS mounts the box in liv'ry coat.

Scenes odd as these, if CLOE can endure,
(And yet these scenes are town in miniature)
Come and reflect on Ranelagh with scorn,
Content ev'n here, at least 'till routs return.

ON A
FIT of the GOUT.

By the Same.

WHerefore was man thus form'd with eye sublime,
    With active joints, to traverse hill or plain,
But to contemplate nature in her prime,
    Lord of this ample world, his fair domain?
Why on this various earth such beauty pour'd,
But for thy pleasure, man, her sovereign lord?

Why does the mantling vine her juice afford,
    Nectareous, but to cheer with cordial taste?
Why are the earth and air and ocean stor'd
    With beast, fish, fowl; if not for man's repast?
Yet what avails to me, or taste, or sight,
Exil'd from every object of delight?

So

So much I feel of anguish, day and night
    Tortur'd, benumb'd; in vain the fields to range
Me vernal breezes, and mild suns invite:
    In vain the banquet smokes with kindly change
Of delicacies, while on every plate
Pain lurks in ambush, and alluring fate.

Fool! not to know the friendly powers create
    These maladies in pity to mankind:
These abdicated reason reinstate,
    When lawless appetite usurps the mind;
Heaven's faithful centries at the door of bliss
Plac'd to deter, or to chastise excess.

Weak is the aid of wisdom to repress
    Passion perverse; philosophy how vain!
'Gainst Circe's cup, enchanting sorceress;
    Or when the Syren sings her warbling strain.
Whate'er or sages teach, or bards reveal,
Men still are men, and learn but when they feel.

As in some free and well-pois'd common-weal
    Sedition warns the rulers how to steer,
As storms and thunders rattling with loud peal,
    From noxious dregs the dull horizon clear;
So when the mind imbrutes in sloth supine,
Sharp pangs awake her energy divine.

Cease then, ah cease, fond mortal, to repine
  At laws, which nature wisely did ordain;
Pleasure, what is it? rightly to define,
  'Tis but a short-liv'd interval from pain:
Or rather each alternately renew'd,
Gives to our lives a sweet vicissitude.

Horace, Ode XIV. Book I. imitated in 1746.

By the Same.

O Ship! shall new waves again bear thee to sea?
  Where, alas! art thou driving? keep steady to shore,
Thy sides are left without an oar,
And thy shaken mast groans, to rude tempests a prey.
  Thy tackle all torn, can no longer endure
The assaults of the surge that now triumphs and reigns,
  None of thy sails entire remains,
Nor a God to protect in another sad hour.
  Though thy outside bespeaks thee of noble descent,
The forests chief pride, yet thy race and thy fame,
  What are they but an empty name?
Wise mariners trust not to gilding and paint.
  Beware then lest Thou float, uncertain again,
The sport of wild winds; late my sorrowful care,
  And now my fondest wish, beware
Of the changeable shoals where the Rhine meets the Main.

The

The Female Right to LITERATURE, in a Letter to a young Lady from FLORENCE.

By THOMAS SEWARD, M. A.

Whilst you, ATHENIA, with assiduous toil
Reap the rich fruits of learning's fertile soil;
Now search whate'er historic truth hath shewn,
And make the wealth of ages past your own;
Now crop the blossoms of poetic flow'rs,
And range delighted in the Muses' bow'rs;
Say, will the sweetest of her sex attend
To lines by friendship, not by flatt'ry penn'd;
To lines which tempt not worth with empty praise;
But to still greater height that worth would raise;
To lines which dare against a world decide,
And stem the rage of custom's rapid tide?
  Come then, ATHENIA, freely let us scan
The coward insults of that tyrant, man.
Self-prais'd, and grasping at despotic pow'r,
He looks on slav'ry as the female dow'r;
To Nature's boon ascribes what force has giv'n,
And usurpation deems the gift of heav'n.
See the first-peopled East, where ASIA sheds
Her balmy spices o'er her fertile meads:

There,

There, while th' ASSYRIAN ſtretch'd his wide domain
From diſtant Indus to the Cyprian main,
All nature's laws by impious force were broke;
The female ſex to ſlav'ry's galling yoke
Bow'd their fair necks: from ſocial life confin'd,
And all th' exertions of the enlighten'd mind,
Clos'd in a proud Seraglio's wanton bow'rs,
The dalliance of a tyrant's looſer hours.
By kings' examples ſubjects form their lives,
Dependent ſatraps had their train of wives;
Proportion'd pow'r each petty tyrant craves,
And each poor female was the ſlave of ſlaves.

When PERSIA next o'erturn'd th' Aſſyrian throne,
Deſtroy'd her tyranny and fix'd its own;
The fair diſtreſs'd no milder treatment ſaw,
This was indeed *th' unalterable law.*
In future times, whatever maſters came,
Tyrants were chang'd, but tyranny the ſame.
At length t' accumulate the female woes,
The grand impoſtor MAHOMET aroſe;
Swoln with prophetic lyes, he lay'd his plan
On the firm baſis of the pride of man;
" Women, the toys of men, and ſlaves of luſt,
" Are but meer moulds to form man's outward cruſt;
" The heavenly ſpark, that animates the clay,
" Of the prime eſſence that effulgent ray,
" Th' immortal ſoul, is all to man confin'd,
" Not meanly ſquander'd on weak woman-kind."

Accurſed

Accurfed wretch! by hell's black council driv'n
Thus to debafe the faireft work of heav'n.
And could Religion rear her facred head
Fraught with fuch doctrines? could fuch errors fpread
From weftern TANGIER, and the fun-burnt Moor,
To the cold TARTAR's ever-frozen fhore?
Ev'n GREECE too not exempt, GREECE, once the feat
Where Senfe and Freedom held the reins of ftate;
Where Force was Reafon's hand-maid; where the bands
Of Love and Friendfhip join'd the wedded hands;
Where flourifh'd once, and flourifh ftill in fame
Th' ATHENIAN matron, and the SPARTAN dame.

In ROME too Liberty once reign'd, in ROME
The female virtues were allow'd to bloom,
And bloom they did: when CANNÆ's fatal plain
Was heap'd with mountains of the Roman flain,
Was there a matron wept her children *dead?*
Was there a matron wept not thofe that *fled?*
Then when each rumour feem'd the voice of fate,
And fpoke the victor thund'ring at their gate,
Was there one mention'd peace? did they not pour
Their wealth, their jewels, to the public ftore,
In emulous hafte all preffing to be poor?

Alas how chang'd! how are the mighty funk,
From the firm Patriot to the whining Monk!
Where Induftry fecur'd the public good,
Where cenfors, confuls, and dictators plough'd,

Now lazy zealots batten on the spoil,
And consecrated Sloth devours the farmer's toil.
But oh still worse! where Love and Friendship shone,
Domestic Tyranny has fix'd his throne,
With all his train of monsters: at his side,
Swoln with self-flatteries, sits stiff-neck'd Pride;
Two twin-born fiends his other ear engage,
Heart-canker'd Jealousy, and fire-ey'd Rage;
In front, his empire's sole support and source,
Rattling chains, bars, and locks, stalks brutal Force;
Whilst pale and shrivel'd, crouch'd beneath the chair,
Lies sneaking, conscious Worthlesness; and near
Squint-ey'd Suspicion lurks, with self-distracting Fear.

   Hail, happy BRITAIN, dear parental land,
Where Liberty maintains her latest stand!
Oh while amidst tyrannic realms I rove,
Enamour'd let me pour my filial love
Into thy bosom. When the raven wings
Of darkness hover o'er me, when the springs
Of every outward sense are shut, my soul
Thee oft revisits, oft without controul
Ranges thy fields delighted, and inhales
Friendship's pure joys, and Freedom's healthful gales.

   But say, BRITANNIA, do thy sons, who claim
A birth-right liberty, dispense the same
In equal scales? Why then does Custom bind
In chains of Ignorance the female mind?

Why is to them the bright ethereal ray
Of science veil'd ? Why does each pedant say,
" Shield me, propitious powers, nor clog my life
" With that supreme of plagues *a learned wife*.
" 'Tis man's with science to expand the soul,
" And wing his eagle-flight from pole to pole ;
" 'Tis his to pierce antiquity's dark gloom,
" And the still thicker shades of times to come ;
" 'Tis his to guide the pond'rous helm of state,
" And bear alone all wisdom's solid weight.
" Let woman with alluring graces move
" The fondling passions and the baby love ;
" Be this our only science, be her doom
" Fix'd to the toilette, the spinnet and loom."

 Tongue-doughty pedant, was ATHENIA's soul
Form'd for these only ? Bring th' exactest rule
Of judgment to the tryal, prove that e'er
Thy school-proud tribe engross'd a greater share
Of mental excellence ; though vernal Youth
Just swells her lovely bosom, yet blest Truth,
Offspring of Sense and Industry, has there
Long fix'd her residence ; and taught the fair
Or wisdom's deep recesses to explore,
Or on invention's rapid wings to soar
Above th' Aonian mount ; and canst thou think
That virtues, which exalt the soul, can sink
The outward charms ? must knowledge give offence ?
And are the graces all at war with sense ?

Say,

Say, who of all the fair is form'd to move
The fondest passions, most ecstatic love,
More than ATHENIA? in her gentle eye
Soft innocence and virgin modesty
Incessant shine, while still a new-born grace
Springs in each speaking feature of her face.
Her sprightly wit no forward pertness spoils;
No self-assuming air her judgment soils;
Still prone to learn, though capable to teach,
And lofty all her thoughts, but humble all her speech.
Proceed, ATHENIA, let thy growing mind
Take every knowledge in of every kind;
Still on perfection fix thy steady eye,
Be ever rising, rise thou ne'er so high.
But oh reflect, that in th' advent'rous flight,
Thou mount'st a glorious, but a dangerous height;
When every science, every grace shall join,
When most thy wit, when most thy beauties shine,
When thickest crowds enamour'd press around,
When loudest every tongue thy praise shall sound,
When verse too offers incense to thy shrine,
And adoration breathes in every line,
Then let my friendly Muse express her care,
Then most will danger spread her viewless snare;
Then let this truth possess thy inmost soul,
" One drop of Vanity may spoil the whole."

 Not self-secure on earth can Knowledge dwell,
Knowledge the bliss of heav'n and pang of hell,

Alike

Alike the inſtrument of good and evil,
The attribute of God and of the Devil.
Without her, Virtue is a powerleſs Will;
She, without Virtue, is a powerfull ill;
Does ſhe then join with Virtue, or oppoſe,
She proves the beſt of Friends, or worſt of Foes.
O! be they once in happieſt union join'd,
And be that union in ATHENIA's mind.

On SHAKSPEARE's Monument at Stratford upon Avon.

By the Same.

GREAT HOMER's birth ſev'n rival cities claim,
  Too mighty ſuch monopoly of Fame;
Yet not to birth alone did HOMER owe
His wond'rous worth; what EGYPT could beſtow,
With all the ſchools of GREECE and ASIA join'd,
Enlarg'd th' immenſe expanſion of his mind.
Nor yet unrival'd the MÆONIAN ſtrain,
The [a] Britiſh Eagle, and the Mantuan Swan
Tow'r equal heights. But happier STRATFORD, thou
With inconteſted laurels deck thy brow:
Thy Bard was thine *unſchool'd*, and from thee brought
More than all EGYPT, GREECE, or ASIA taught.
Not HOMER's ſelf ſuch matchleſs honours won;
The Greek has Rivals, but thy SHAKSPEARE none.

[a] Milton.

A SONG.

A SONG.

By the Same.

I.

WHEN fair SERENA first I knew,
   By friendship's happy union charm'd;
Incessant joys around her flew,
   And gentle smiles my bosom warm'd.

II.

But when with fond officious care,
   I press'd to breathe my amorous pain,
Her lips spoke nought but cold despair,
   Her eyes shot ice through every vein.

III.

Thus in ITALIA's lovely vales
   The sun his genial vigour yields,
Reviving heat each sense regales,
   And plenty crowns the smiling fields.

IV.

When nearer we approach his ray,
   High on the Alps' stupendous brow,
Surpriz'd we see pale sun-beams play
   On everlasting hills of snow.

CHISWICK.

CHISWICK.

By the Same.

THE potent Lord, that this bright villa plann'd,
Exhibits here a *Paradise regain'd*;
Whate'er of Verdure have Hills, Lawns, or Woods,
Whate'er of Splendor, Buildings, Flow'rs, or Floods,
Whate'er of Fruits the Trees, of Birds the Air,
In blissful union are collected here:
All with such harmony dispos'd, as shews,
That in the midst the *Tree of Knowledge* grows.

The INDIFFERENT.

From the Italian of Metastasio.

By the Same.

THANKS, CLOE, thy coquetting art
At length hath heal'd my love-sick heart,
At length thy slave is free;
I feel no tyrant's proud controul,
I feel no inmate in my soul,
But peace and liberty.

No longer now a fierce desire
In anger masks its amorous fire,
   And fiercer burns suppress'd:
I blush not when thy name I hear,
I meet thee suddenly, and fear
   No fluttering in my breast.

In dreams I every trifle see,
Yet very rarely dream of thee:
   I wake, nor think about thee:
When absent I ne'er wish thee near:
And when thou'rt present I nor fear,
   Nor pray to be without thee.

I think, hear, talk about thy charms,
Nor stoop the head, nor fold the arms;
   Nay ev'n my wrongs sit easy.
And when my favour'd rival's near,
And eyes me with insulting leer,
   His triumphs never teaze me.

Put on thy looks of cold disdain,
Or speak respectful, 'tis in vain,
   Nor frowns nor smiles can move.
Those lips no more have words that bind,
Those eyes no more have light to find
   The path that leads to love.

Seasons,

Seasons, which wont to take their dye
Of foul or fair, from CLOE's eye,
   Now their own livery wear.
This place I hate, and that I love,
The fen's a fen, the grove's a grove,
   If absent thou, or there.

Judge if I speak like one sincere,
Still I confess your face is fair,
   But so are twenty faces;
And if plain truth will not offend,
You've now some features I could mend,
   Which once appear'd all graces.

Nay more, I own, when from my heart
I strove to tug the fatal dart,
   It cut my heart in sunder:
But to relieve a constant pain,
And to retrieve one's self again,
   What would one not go-under?

The fluttering bird in viscous snare
Entangled, willingly will spare
   For liberty a feather;
In time again the feather grows,
And wise by danger made, he knows
   To shun the snare for ever.

But still I hear you smiling say,
'Tis sign you've flung your chains away,
   You take such pains to shew 'em.
Why, CLOE, there's a fond delight
Our former dangers to recite,
   And let our neighbours know 'em.

After the thunder of the wars,
The veteran thus displays his scars,
   And tells you of his pains;
The galley-slave, enslav'd no more,
Shews you the shackles which he wore,
   And where their mark remains.

I talk, 'cause talking gives delight,
I please myself not CLOE by't,
   Nor care if she believe;
And when myself she deigns to name,
Whether she praise my song or blame,
   I neither joy nor grieve.

For me I quit a fickle fair,
CLOE has lost a heart sincere,
   Who first should sing *Te Deum?*
You'll never find so true a swain;
But women full as false and vain,
   By dozens one may see 'em.

The Triumph of INDIFFERENCE.

Being the same ODE, imitated by an unknown Hand.

I.

THANKS, dear coquet! indulgent cheat!
  Kind heaven, and your more kind deceit,
    At length have set me free;
No more I sigh, and doat, and pine,
All ease without, and calm within,
    In peace and liberty.

II.

Cupid no more has power to scorch,
Time sure has robb'd him of his torch,
  Ne'er was a cooler creature:
That name no more has such eclat,
No more my heart goes pit-a-pat
  At sight of each dear feature.

III.

I sleep at night, and sometimes dream,
Nor you the fond vexatious theme;
  I wake, nor think about you:
I meet, I leave you, meet again,
But feel no mighty joy or pain,
  Or with you, or without you.

IV.

Now with indifference I chat
Of eyes, lips, bubbies, and all that,
  And laugh at former follies:
Joke with my rival when we meet,
What eye so keen! what lips so sweet!
  What skin so soft as Molly's!

V.

Leave then those little torturing arts,
You practise on complying hearts;
  They're all in vain, believe me:
Whether those eyes look kind, or weep,
The pouting, or the smiling lip,
  Will neither please, nor grieve me.

VI.

From those despotic looks, no more
(Once tyrants of each fickle hour)
  I date my grief and joy:
May, though you frown, looks sweetly clad;
And dull December's mighty sad,
  Though you stand smiling by.

VII.

Yet still (for I am quite sincere)
You're mighty pretty,—true, my dear;
  But, like your pretty sex,
You've here and there, and now and then
A failing; for like other men,
  I now can spy defects.

VIII.

Yet once with coward fondness curs'd,
My poor weak heart I fear'd would burst
  At thought of separation:
But now despise my feeble chain,
And bless the salutary pain
  That cur'd me of my passion.

IX.

'Impatient of his iron cage,
The bird thus spends his little rage,
  And 'scapes with shatter'd wings:
But soon with new-fledg'd pinions soars,
And hast'ning to his native bow'rs,
  A joyful welcome sings.

X.

Fond female vanity will say,
These long harangues they sure betray
  A heart that's hankering still:
This passion so proclaim'd in song,
This tale so pleasing to the tongue,
  Does it not touch the will?

XI.

Lovers, like soldiers, Molly, dwell
With pleasure on the horrid tale,
  When all the danger's o'er:
Like other slaves from fetters free,
We smile with anxious joy, to see
  The chains which once we wore.

XII.

In kind indulgence to a heart,
Engag'd in so severe a part,
  This sweet revenge I write;
Rail, weep, be woman all, for I
Lull'd in indifference, defy
  Your fondness or your spite.

XIII.

A frail false maid I lost, but you
A man, fond, generous, and true;
  Which fortune is the worse?
Try all love's mighty empire round,
A faithful lover's seldom found;
  A jilt's a common curse.

The SHEPHERD'S FAREWELL to his LOVE.
Being the same ODE.
Translated by Mr. RODERICK *.

PHœbe, thank thy false heart, it has fix'd my repose,
  The gods have had pity at length on my woes;
I feel it, I feel my soul loose from its chain,
And at last freedom comes, often dream'd of in vain.

---

* Richard Roderick, Fellow of Magdalen College in Cambridge and of the Royal and Antiquarian Societies. He assisted Mr. Edwards in compiling the Canons of Criticism, and died 20 July 1756.

The flame is burnt out, and each paffion at reft,
Under which love difguis'd ftill might lurk in my breaft;
No more, when thou'rt nam'd, the warm blufhes arife,
No more flutters my heart, when I meet with your eyes.

In my fleep now no longer thy image I fee,
Nor the firft of my thoughts, when I wake, is of thee;
When from thee, no more of thy abfence I plain,
When with thee, I feel neither pleafure nor pain.

My heart without fondnefs can mufe on thy charms,
My paft pains I recount, yet no paffion alarms;
Difcompos'd I'm no longer, when tow'rd me you move,
And at eafe with my rival I talk of my love.

Whether haughty thy frown, whether gentle thy ftrain,
In vain thy proud looks, thy fond fpeeches in vain;
Thy falfe tongue to beguile me no more has the art,
No more thy keen eye knows the way to my heart.

Whether penfive or cheerful, no longer to you
For this are my thanks, or for that my blame due:
The gay profpect now pleafes, though you are away,
And your prefence no more can make drearinefs gay.

Believe me, I ftill can allow that thou'rt fair,
But not that no fair-one can with thee compare;

X 3 And

And though beauteous I own thee, yet still in thy face
I can now spy a fault, which I once thought a grace.

When first the fix'd arrow I pluck'd from my heart,
Oh, methought I should die! so severe was the smart:
But from pow'r so oppressive to set myself clear,
Torments greater than dying with patience I'd bear.

When lim'd the poor bird thus with eagerness strains,
Nor regrets the lost plume, so his freedom he gains;
The loss of his plumage small time will restore,
And once try'd the false twig, it can cheat him no more.

The old flame, never flatter yourself to believe,
While it dwells on my tongue, in my heart still must live;
Our dangers, when past, with delight we repeat,
What in suffering was pain, to remembrance is sweet.

'Tis thus when the soldier returns from the wars,
He fights o'er his old battles, and vaunts of his scars:
With pleasure the captive, his liberty gain'd,
The fetters thus shows, which once held him enchain'd.

Thus I talk, and I still will talk on while I may,
Nor heed I, though you disbelieve what I say:
I ask not that Phœbe my talk should approve,
Let her too, if she can, talk at ease of my love.

An inconstant I leave, a true lover you lose;
Which first of us two will have comfort, who knows?
This I know—Phœbe ne'er such a true love will find;
I can easily meet with a fair as unkind.

RIDDLE.

By the Same.

Through the close covert of the shady grove,
  One summer's day it was my chance to rove,
Where, shrouded from the sun's too scorching ray,
Stretch'd at her ease, half-slumbering Cloe lay.
Occasion so inviting, who could miss?
Softly I stole, and snatch'd a sudden kiss.
Startled at first, the rising blush display'd
The quick resentment of the ruffled maid;
Lively display'd—for soon it over past;
Such blushing anger never long did last!
Quick reconcilement must to rage succeed,
Where wrongs ideal solid pleasures breed.
Submissive looks my pardon soon obtain'd,
And pardon'd love as soon new boldness gain'd.
Offending thus, forgiving thus, we lay,
Long time entranc'd with the alternate play;

'Till

'Till warn'd, too soon, by envious night, we part:
The thrilling joy still flutters round my heart;
Thought still, though fainter, paints the glowing bliss,
On fancy's lip still cleaves the rapt'rous kiss.
　　But mark the sad effects of casual love,
And tread with caution in the shady grove.
In due time, Cloe at my doors appears,
A fix'd composure on her brow she wears;
And guess the cause: close in her lap conceal'd
A lovely twin in either hand she held;
And take, she cry'd, these pledges of our love,
These fruits you planted in the shady grove.
　　Soft as the downy bloom on Cloe's cheek,
Smooth as the polish'd ivory of her neck,
Warm as her bosom, white as was her arm,
So smooth were they and white, so soft and warm.
Pleas'd I receiv'd them for the giver's sake,
Heedless what censures strait-lac'd prudes might make.
　　Compliant to my forming hand they grew,
And with their size increas'd obedience due.
As I direct they take th' appointed bent,
With every motion, every beck, consent;
Whate'er I want, they reach with ready hand,
Where-e'er I go, they wait at my command.
Now at his ease one in my bosom lays;
While by my side the other wanton plays;
Now this my hand embraces, t'other free,
Takes his full swing and plays at liberty.

　　　　　　　　　　　　　　　　Before

Before me hand in hand sometimes they move,
Emblems of friendship, and united love;
Sometimes behind my leading steps they trace,
Still closely knit in brotherly embrace;
Anon on either side as guards attend,
At once adorn me, and at once defend.
Still more and more my love they thus engage,
Thus still shall cherish my declining age;
And when th' appointed hour of fate shall come,
They'll follow still attendant on my tomb.
More lasting far than man's soon-fading breath,
Their love extends beyond the vale of death;
They'll hang for ever o'er my much-lov'd bust,
'Till they themselves, like me, are turn'd to dust.

RIDDLE.

———— Mortalis in unum
Quodque caput, vultu mutabilis, albus an ater.

By the Same.

TORN from the fruitful spot on which I grew,
  Me innocent unnumber'd pains pursue;
Pains more afflicting, as from man they flow,
From parent man! for birth to man I owe.
Sometimes on spikes of steel my nerves they rend,
Sometimes asunder split from end to end;

In

In boiling cauldrons now immers'd I lie,
New doom'd the rage of drying fires to try:
There while in double torment scorch'd and drown'd,
Fast tied I writhe the rigid stake around.
Last their fierce hate its utmost effort tries
With all Barbarian pomp of sacrifice.
The purple fillet round my temples wreathes,
From every part the scented unguent breathes;
O'er my white locks the sacred flower is spread,
Whilst on the fatal block is plac'd my head.
Yet with fix'd constancy I bear my doom;
And constancy at last will overcome.
From all my tryals I return at length,
My worth increas'd, my beauty, and my strength.
The suffering martyr thus in torment dies,
In sainted state more glorious to arise.
And now I re-assume my native state,
My torturers now beneath their burden sweat,
Slaves in their turn to me, and think it pride
If on their subject necks I deign to ride.
 Yet still my filial duty I retain,
Unchang'd by honours, as unmov'd by pain.
Still to mankind a friend, I daily shed
My warmest blessings on his parent head;
Around him still with fond embraces twine,
As round the elm her tendrils curls the vine.
Nor quit him e'er till he to rest repairs,
And every morn renew my constant cares.

           Ready

Ready alike on rich and poor to wait;
I suit myself to every different state.
With priest in whitish dress array'd I shine,
Emblem of purity and truth divine.
His solemn face the doctor owes to me,
His solemn face, to which he owes his fee.
At bench or bar, I add a dignity
To th' upright sentence, or rhetoric plea;
Hence without me no judge explains the laws,
Nor coifed council pleads the puzzling cause:
In fullest floods my bounty showers on them
Profuse, descending to the garment's hem.
Gorgeous in silken garb I grace the beau;
And all around ambrosial fragrance throw;
Nor less decorous, though with dust o'erspread,
When to the camp the valiant warriors lead,
Gorgonian terrors to each mien I add,
And still their weakest part with care I shade.

RIDDLE.

RIDDLE.

By the Same.

MY ſize is large, my ſhape's uncouth,
   I have neither limb nor feature;
Men's hands have form'd my ſkin ſo ſmooth:
   My guts were made by nature.

Nor male nor female is my ſex,
   You'll ſcarce believe my troth:
For when I've told you all my tricks
   You'll ſwear 't muſt needs be both.

For oft my maſter lies with me,
   His wife I oft enjoy;
Yet ſhe's no whore, no cuckold he,
   And true to both am I.

My cloaths, nor women fit, nor men,
   They're neither coat nor gown;
Yet oft both men and maidens, when
   They're naked, have them on.

When I'm upon my legs, I lie,
  Yet legs in truth I have none;
And never am I seen so high
  To rise as when I'm down.

What's oft my belly is oft my back,
  And what my feet, my head;
And though I'm up, I have a knack
  Of being still a-bed.

Audivere, Lyce, &c. HOR. BOOK IV. Ode 13.
IMITATED.

By the Same.

LYCE, at length my vows are heard,
  My vows so oft to heaven preferr'd;
Welcome thy silver'd hairs!
[a] In vain thy affectation gay,
To hide the manifest decay,
  In vain thy youthful airs.

———[a] fis anus, et tamen
Vis formosa videri
Ludisque ———

If still thy cheeks preserve a blush,
With [b] heat of wine, not youth, they flush,
  [c] Unamiable stain!
If still thou warblest; harsh the note
When [d] trembling age shakes in the throat
  Th' involuntary strain.

Think'st thou can these my love prolong?
(Ungrateful blush! untuneful song!)
  Or rival Hebe's charms?
Hebe melodious, Hebe fair,
For [e] judgment swells her rapt'rous air,
  For [f] youth her blushes warms.

The rosy cheek, the forehead smooth,
Those native ornaments of youth,
  Once lost, are lost for aye.
No art can smooth [g], no paint repair
The furrow'd face; [h] no diamond's glare
  Give lustre to decay.

    ——————et [b] bibis impudens.
    Cantu [d] tremulo [b] pota Cupidinem
    [e] Lentum solicitas————
    ——————[f] virentis et
    [e] Doctæ psallere Chiæ
      Pulchris excubat in genis.
    Nec [g] Coæ referunt jam tibi purpuræ,
    Nec [h] clari lapides, tempora quæ semel
      Notis condita fastis
        Inclusit volucris dies.

What now of all which once was thine,
[i] Feature, [k] Complexion, [l] Mien divine,
Remains the ſenſe to charm ?
[m] Why now command they not my love ?
Once could they—[n] even though Cloe ſtrove
Their empire to diſarm.

Cloe !—alas, thou much-lov'd name !
[o] Thou, full of beauty, full of fame,
Found'ſt an untimely urn !
[p] Whilſt Lyce, reft of every grace
T' inrich the mind, t' adorn the face,
Still lives, the public ſcorn [q].

Quo [i] Venus fugit, ah ! quove [k] color decens,
Quo [l] motus ? quid habes illius, illius,
Quæ ſpirabat amores ?
[m] Quæ me ſurpuerat mihi ?
[n] Fælix poſt Cynaram.
————[o] ſed Cynaræ breves
Annos fata dedere :
Servatura diu [p] parem
Cornicis vetulæ temporibus Lycen.

[q] The contemptuous ſatire at the concluſion of the original, is preſerved in the Engliſh, but a graver turn is given to it, inſtead of the more ludicrous one of Horace. Whether judiciouſly or no, may be better determined by any body, than by the author.

A SON-

A SONNET.

Imitated from the Spanish of LOPEZ DE VEGA.
Menagiana tom. iv. p. 176.

By the Same.

CAPRICIOUS Wray a Sonnet needs must have;
   I ne'er was so put to't before :——a Sonnet!
  Why, fourteen verses must be spent upon it;
'Tis good howe'er t' have conquer'd the first stave.

Yet I shall ne'er find rhymes enough by half,
   Said I, and found myself i' th' midst o' the second.
  If twice four verses were but fairly reckon'd,
I should turn back on th' hardest part and laugh.

Thus far with good success I think I've scribbled,
   And of the twice seven lines have clean got o'er ten.
Courage! another 'll finish the first triplet.
   Thanks to thee, Muse, my work begins to shorten.
There's thirteen lines got through driblet by driblet.
    'Tis done! count how you will, I warr'nt there's
      fourteen.

SONNETS.

By T. EDWARDS, Esq [a].

SONNET I.

To PHILIP YORKE, Esq; now earl of Hardwicke.

O Yorke, whom virtue makes the worthy heir
   Of Hardwicke's titles, and of Kent's [b] estate,
Blest in a wife, whose beauty, though so rare,
   Is the least grace of all that round her wait.

---

[a] Thomas Edwards, Esq; was a Barrister of Lincoln's Inn, and the son and grandson of two gentlemen, who had practised the law with success. He was educated at Eton, from whence he removed to King's College, Cambridge; after which he settled in Lincoln's Inn. He spent the last seventeen years of his life principally at Turrick in Buckinghamshire; but died while on a visit to Mr. Richardson, at Parson's Green, 3d of January 1757, aged 58 years. He was the author of *The Canons of Criticism*.

[b] Lord Hardwicke married Lady Jemima Campbell, only daughter of John Earl of Breadalbin, by the Lady Amabel Grey, eldest daughter and co-heir of Henry de Grey, Duke of Kent.

While other youths, sprung from the good and great,
  In devious paths of pleasure seek their bane,
Reckless of wisdom's lore, of birth, or state,
  Meanly debauch'd, or insolently vain;

Through Virtue's sacred gate to Honour's fane
  You and your fair associate ceaseless climb
With glorious emulation, sure to gain
  A meed, shall last beyond the reign of Time:
From your example long may Britain see,
  Degenerate Britain, what the Great should be!

SONNET II.

To JOHN CLERKE, Esq.

Wisely, O Clerke, enjoy the present hour,
  The present hour is all the time we have,
High God the rest has plac'd beyond our pow'r,
  Consign'd, perhaps, to grief—or to the grave.

Wretched the man, who toils ambition's slave;
  Who pines for wealth, or sighs for empty fame;
Who rolls in pleasures which the mind deprave,
  Bought with severe remorse, and guilty shame.

Virtue

Virtue and knowledge be our better aim;
   These help us Ill to bear, or teach to shun;
Let Friendship cheer us with her gen'rous flame,
   Friendship, the sum of all our joys in one:
So shall we live each moment fate has giv'n;
How long, or short, let us resign to heav'n.

SONNET III.

To FRANCIS KNOLLYS, Esq.

O Sprung from worthies, who with counsels wise
   Adorn'd and strengthen'd great Elisa's throne [a]
Who yet with virtuous pride, may'st well despise
   To borrow praise from merits not thy own.

Oft as I view the monumental stone
   Where our lov'd Harrison's cold ashes rest,
Musing on joys with him long past and gone,
   A pleasing sad remembrance fills my breast.—

---

[a] He was descended from Sir Francis Knollys, Knight of the Garter, and treasurer of the household to Queen Elizabeth.

Did the sharp pang we feel for friends deceas'd
  Unbated last, we must with anguish die;
But nature bids its rigour should be eas'd
  By lenient time, and strong necessity:
These calm the passions, and subdue the mind
To bear th' appointed lot of human kind.

SONNET IV.

To Mr. CRUSIUS.

CRUSIUS, I hop'd the little heaven shall spare
  Of my short day, which flits away so fast,
And sickness threats with clouds to overcast,
In social converse oft with thee to share.

Ill-luck for me, that wayward fate should tear
  Thee from the haven thou had'st gain'd at last,
  Again to try the toils and dangers past
In foreign climates, and an hostile air:

Yet duteous to thy country's call attend,
  Which claims a portion of thy useful years,
And back with speed thy course to Britain bend:
If, ere again we meet, perchance should end
  My dark'ning eve, thou'lt pay some friendly tears,
Grateful to him, who liv'd and dy'd thy friend.

SONNET V.

On a FAMILY-PICTURE.

WHEN pensive on that portraiture I gaze,
  Where my four brothers round about me stand,
And four fair sisters smile with graces bland,
The goodly monument of happier days;

And think, how soon insatiate death, who preys
  On all, has cropp'd the rest with ruthless hand,
  While only I survive of all that band,
Which one chaste bed did to my father raise;

It seems, that like a column left alone,
  The tott'ring remnant of some splendid fane,
    'Scap'd from the fury of the barb'rous Gaul,
And wasting Time, which has the rest o'erthrown,
  Amidst our house's ruins I remain,
    Single, unprop'd, and nodding to my fall.

SONNET VI.

To JOHN REVETT, Esq.

REVETT, who well hast judg'd the task too hard,
   Of this short life throughout the total day
   To follow glory's false bewitching ray,
Through certain toils, uncertain of reward;

A prince's service how should we regard?
   As service still—though deck'd in livery gay,
   Disguis'd with titles, gilded o'er with pay,
Specious, yet ill to liberty preferr'd.

Bounding thy wishes by the golden mean,
   Nor weakly bartering happiness for show,
Wisely thou'st left the busy bustling scene,
Where merit seldom has successful been,
   In Checquer's shades to taste the joys, that flow
From calm retirement, and a mind serene.

SONNET VII.

To RICHARD OWEN CAMBRIDGE, Esq.

Cambridge, with whom, my pilot and my guide,
  Pleas'd I have travers'd thy Sabrina's flood,
Both where she foams impetuous foil'd with mud,
And where she peaceful rolls her golden tide.

Never, O never let ambition's pride
  (Too oft pretexted with our country's good)
    And tinsel'd pomp, despis'd when understood,
Or thirst of wealth thee from her banks divide.

Reflect how calmly, like her infant wave,
  Flows the clear current of a private life;
    See the wide public stream by tempests toss'd
Of every changing wind the sport, or slave,
  Soil'd with corruption, vex'd with party strife,
    Cover'd with wrecks of peace and honour lost.

SONNET VIII.

On the CANTOS of SPENSER's Fairy Queen, lost in the Passage from Ireland.

WO worth the man, who in ill hour assay'd
   To tempt that western frith with vent'rous keel,
And seek what heav'n, regardful of our weal,
Had hid in fogs, and night's eternal shade.

Ill-starr'd Hibernia! well art thou repaid
   For all the woes that Britain made thee feel,
   By Henry's wrath, and Pembroke's conqu'ring steel,
Who sack'd thy towns, and castles disarray'd:

Nor longer now with idle sorrow mourn
   Thy plunder'd wealth, or liberties restrain'd,
     Nor deem their victories thy loss or shame;
Severe revenge on Britain in thy turn
   And ample spoils thy treach'rous waves obtain'd,
     Which sunk one half of Spenser's deathless fame.

SONNET IX.

To the Memory of Mrs. M. PAICE.

PEACE to thy ashes, to thy mem'ry fame,
   Bright paragon of merit feminine,
In forming whom kind nature did inshrine
A mind angelic in a faultless frame;

Through every stage of changing life the same,
   How did thy bright example ceaseless shine,
   And every grace with every virtue join
To raise the virgin's and the matron's name!

In thee, religion, cheerful and serene,
   Unsour'd by superstition, spleen, or pride,
   Through all the social offices of life
To shed its genuine influence was seen;
   This thy chief ornament, thy surest guide,
   This form'd the daughter, parent, friend, and wife.

SONNET X.

To the Author of [a] Observations on the Conversion and Apostleship of St. PAUL.

O Lyttelton, great meed shalt thou receive,
   Great meed of fame, thou and thy learn'd compeer [b],
   Who 'gainst the sceptic's doubt, and scorner's sneer,
Assert those heav'n-born truths, which you believe.

In elder times thus heroes wont t' atchieve
   Renown, they held the faith of JESUS dear,
   And round their ivy-crown, or laurell'd spear,
Blush'd not religion's olive branch to weave.

Thus Raleigh, thus immortal Sidney shone
   (Illustrious names) in great Elisa's days.
Nor doubt his promise firm, that such who own
In evil times, undaunted, though alone,
   His glorious truth, such he will crown with praise,
And glad agnize before his Father's throne.

[a] George Lyttelton, Esq; afterwards Lord Lyttelton.
[b] Gilbert West, Esq; who just before had published "Observations on the History and Evidence of the Resurrection of Jesus Christ."

SONNET XI.

On the Death of Miss J. M.

Young, fair, and good! ah why should young and fair
   And good be huddled in untimely grave?
Must so sweet flow'r so brief a period have,
Just bloom and charm, then fade and disappear?

Yet our's the loss, who ill, alas! can spare
   The bright example, which thy virtues gave;
   The guerdon thine, whom gracious heav'n did save
From longer trial in this vale of care.

Rest then, sweet saint, in peace and honour rest,
   While our true tears bedew thy maiden hearse,
Light lie the earth upon thy lovely breast;
And let a grateful heart with grief oppress'd
   To thy dear mem'ry consecrate this verse,
Though all too mean for who deserves the best.

SONNET XII.

To D. WRAY, Esq.

WRAY, whose dear friendship in the dawning years
   Of undesigning Childhood first began,
Through Youth's gay morn with even tenor ran,
My noon conducted, and my evening cheers,

Rightly dost thou, in whom combin'd appears
   Whate'er for Public Life completes the Man,
   With active Zeal strike out a larger plan,
No useless friend to Senators and Peers:

Me moderate talents and a small estate
   Fit for Retirement's unambitious shade,
     Nor envy I who near approach the throne:
But joyful see thee mingle with the Great,
   See thy deserts with due distinction paid,
     And praise thy lot, contented with my own.

SONNET XIII.

To the Right Hon. Mr. ONSLOW [a], with the foregoing SONNETS.

THOU, who succeffive in that honour'd feat
    Prefid'ft, the feuds of jarring Chiefs to 'fwage,
To check the boift'rous force of party rage,
Raife modeft worth, and guide the high debate,

Sometimes retiring from the toils of State,
    Thou turn'ft th' inftructive Greek or Roman page,
    Or what our Britifh Bards of later age,
In fcarce inferior numbers can relate:

Amid this feaft of Mind, when Fancy's Child,
    Sweet SHAKSPEARE, raps the foul to virtuous deed,
    When SPENSER, warbling tunes his Doric lays,
Or the firft Man from Paradife exil'd
    Great MILTON fings, can aught my ruftic reed
    Prefume to found, that may deferve thy praife?

[a] Arthur Onflow, Efq; Speaker of the Houfe of Commons, afterwards Lord Onflow.

INDEX TO THE SECOND VOLUME.

THE Progress of Love. In four Eclogues	Page 1
Soliloquy of a Beauty	17
Blenheim	20
Epistle to Dr. Ayscough	28
Epistle to Mr. Poyntz	35
Verses under Mr. Poyntz's Picture	39
Epistle to Mr. Pope	40
Epistle to my Lord Hervey	43
Advice to a Lady	46
Song	51
Song	52
Damon and Delia	54
Ode in Imitation of Pastor Fido	56
Part of an Elegy of Tibullus	57
Song	60
Verses written at Mr. Pope's	61
Epigram	62
To Mr. West, at Wickham	63
To Miss Lucy Fortescue	64
To the Same, with Hammond's Elegies	65
To the Same	ibid.

To

To the Same	Page 66
A Prayer to Venus, *in her Temple at* Stowe	67
To the Same. On her pleading Want of Time	68
To the Same	69
To the Same	70
To the Same, with a new Watch	71
An Irregular Ode, written at Wickham *in* 1746	72
To the Memory of the same Lady. A Monody	74
Verses, making Part of an Epitaph on the same Lady	86
On the Abuse of Travelling. A Canto in Imitation of Spenser. *By Mr.* West	88
The Institution of the Order of the Garter. By the Same	113
Epistle to Lord Cornbury	174
An Epistle	193
Epistle to a Lady	206
Epistle to Mr. Pope	213
Epistle to Pollio	215
Ode to William Pultney, *Esq;*	219
Ode to Lord Lonsdale	222
Ode	224
Ode	225
Ode	227
Ode to Mankind	229
Verses to Camilla	237
To Clarissa	239
An Inscription on a Tomb	243
Epigrams	ibid.
The Danger of Writing Verse. By W. Whitehead, *Esq;*	249

To

To the Honourable Charles Townsend, *Esq.*	Page 260
To Mr. Garrick	262
Nature, to Dr. Hoadly	266
The Youth and the Philosopher	268
Ode to a Gentleman on his pitching a Tent, &c.	270
On a Message Card	272
The Je ne sçai Quoi	274
Ode on a distant Prospect of Eton College. *By Mr.* Gray	275
Ode	281
Ode on the Death of a favourite Cat	284
Monody on the Death of Q. Caroline. *By R.* West, *Esq;*	286
A Pipe of Tobacco : in Imitation of six several Authors	293
Ode to the Hon. Charles Yorke, *Esq;*	302
From Cælia to Cloe	304
On a Fit of the Gout	306
An Ode of Horace	308
The female Right to Literature	309
On Shakspeare's *Monument at* Stratford *upon* Avon	315
A Song	316
Chiswick	317
The Indifferent, from the Italian *of* Metastasio	ibid.
The Triumph of Indifference, an Ode	321
The Shepherd's Farewell to his Love	324
Riddles	327, 329, 332
Audivere, Lyce, *&c.*	333
A Sonnet, imitated from the Spanish *of* Lopez de Vega	336
Sonnets	337

The END *of* VOL. II.

www.ingramcontent.com/pod-product-compliance
Lightning Source LLC
Chambersburg PA
CBHW030252240426
43673CB00040B/953